Making God Real for a New Generation

Ministry With Millennials Born From 1982 to 1999

Craig Kennet Miller and MaryJane Pierce Norton

DISCIPLESHIP RESOURCES

PO BOX 340003 • NASHVILLE, TN 37203-0003

www.discipleshipresources.org

Cover and book design by Joey McNair

Edited by Linda R. Whited and Heidi L. Hewitt

ISBN 0-88177-376-X

Library of Congress Control Number 2002103140

DR376

Contents

Top 10 Ways to Use
Making God Real for a New Generation

Now that you have this book, what will you do with it? Here are ten suggestions to ensure that the material in this book is used.

1. Read the book. The information contained here helps you understand who makes up the Millennial Generation, what their world is like, ways you can help them grow in faith, and models of ministry for congregations.

2. List the children and youth in your congregation. Write the names of some of these children and youth in the margins of each chapter. Before or after reading each chapter, pray for the children and youth you have listed.

3. Highlight one or two items from each chapter. Include these tidbits in newsletter articles or as bulletin inserts.

4. Meet with the children and youth of your congregation. Invite them to tell you things the church is doing that they think help them grow in faith. Invite them to suggest other ways they would like their church to help them grow in faith.

5. Use the first session of the study guide with your church council or other administrative body in your congregation. Then evaluate the ministries your congregation provides for children, youth, and young adults.

6. Start a parent study group. Use the study guide to help parents better understand their children and youth.

7. Provide a training session for teachers, small-group leaders, and youth workers. Use the chapters in Section Four, "The Spirituality of Millennials," to help those who work with children, youth, and young adults focus on how the sessions they plan reflect the needs of the Millennial Generation.

8. Select the chapter of most interest to you; then survey children and youth in your community to discover what they think about this subject.

9. Interview the children and youth in your congregation or community using the survey questions on pages 167–70. Compare the results you collect with those of the national study.

10. Use this book as a reference guide. As you plan Sunday school or small-group lessons for children and youth, refer to the material in this book for further information or guidance.

Contributors

Craig Kennet Miller is director of the Center of Evangelism Through New Congregational Development, the General Board of Discipleship, The United Methodist Church, Nashville, Tennessee. He is a specialist in generational studies and is the author of the books *Baby Boomer Spirituality: Ten Essential Values of a Generation, Postmoderns: The Beliefs, Hopes, and Fears of Young Americans (Born 1965–1981),* and *NextChurch.Now: Creating New Faith Communities.*

Interest in the Millennial Generation: "As a person who has written about Baby Boomers and Postmoderns, I find it exciting to learn about this newest generation. I think they have a lot to offer us."

Articles: "A Beginning Point" (pages 9–10), "Section One: Who Are the Millennials?" (pages 13–26), "The Battle for the Hearts and Souls of Preteens" (pages 93–96), "Millennials and Worship" (pages 133–36)

MaryJane Pierce Norton is team leader of Family and Life Span Ministries, the General Board of Discipleship, The United Methodist Church, Nashville, Tennessee. She is the author of the books *Children Worship!* and *Teaching Young Children,* a contributing author for the "What Every Teacher Needs to Know About" series, and coauthor (with Debra Ball-Kilbourne) of the curriculum *FaithHome.*

Interest in the Millennial Generation: "I am fascinated by people—how they grow, develop, interact with others, etc. I am particularly interested in this generation because I have two sons who daily remind me of the needs, wants, and desires of this generation."

Articles: "A Beginning Point" (pages 9–10), "What Families Look Like Today" (pages 29–32), "Growing Through the Life Span" (pages 33–40), "A Family Crisis or Families in Crisis?" (pages 45–52), "Responding to the Needs of Parents" (pages 53–56), "Study Guide" (pages 155–64)

Reginald Blount is instructor of Christian Education and Youth Ministry at Garrett-Evangelical Theological Seminary and director of Faith Passage, a year-long spiritual and leadership development program for high school youth. Reginald is pastor of Trinity African Methodist Episcopal Church in Waukegan, Illinois. He is a candidate in the Garrett-Evangelical/Northwestern University joint program in Religious and Theological Studies, focusing his studies in the areas of Christian education and social ethics.

Interest in the Millennial Generation: "I am an advocate for youth and their issues and concerns, particularly regarding issues of faith and commitment to the gospel of Christ. I desire to work with all persons and faith communities committed to envisioning new and creative ways to minister to, with, and on behalf of youth."

Article: "Faith Passage" (pages 141–44)

Terry B. Carty is director of the Center for Ministries With Young People, the General Board of Discipleship, The United Methodist Church, Nashville, Tennessee. Terry is the author of *Guidelines for Leading Your Congregation: Youth Ministry* (1997–2000 and 2001–2004) and a contributing author for the "What Every Teacher Needs to Know About" series.

Interest in the Millennial Generation: "I have been in local-church youth ministry with Baby Boomers, Postmoderns (a.k.a., GenX), and now Millennials. It is important to understand the forces that drive their culture in order to have more effective ministry with youth."

Articles: "Out-Familying Pseudo-Family Organizations" (pages 57–62), "What Is Success?" (pages 119–23), "Creating a Discipleship System for Youth and Young Adults" (pages 127–32)

Bill Crenshaw is director of Young Adult Ministries, the General Board of Discipleship, The United Methodist Church, Nashville, Tennessee. Bill is a contributing author for the "What Every Teacher Needs to Know About" series, editor of the newsletter *Information: Young Adult Ministries,* and a contributing author to *Christian Home Month* and to *Interpreter* magazine.

Interest in the Millennial Generation: "I am fascinated and challenged by the extraordinary promise this emerging generation of young adults holds for both our culture and the Church of Jesus Christ in America."

Article: "Millennials and Community Service" (pages 115–18)

Dottie Escobedo-Frank is pastor of Community Church of Joy, Glendale, Arizona.

Interest in the Millennial Generation: "I have three children in the Millennial Generation. I am delighted to see this generation embrace its faith in positive ways. This generation is the hope of bringing Christ to the future."

Article: "Who Am I?: Second-Generation Hispanic Americans" (pages 79–82)

John Gooch is a retired clergy member of the Missouri Conference and is engaged in a ministry of writing and training youth leaders. Working from his home in Liberty, Missouri, he writes youth curriculum resources, consults with local churches and annual conferences, and teaches at Perkins School of Youth Ministry. John also works with the senior highs at Liberty First United Methodist Church. He has published several books, including *Claiming the Name: A Theological and Practical Overview of Confirmation* and *Faith Exploration for Older Youth and Young Adults.* He has also written dozens of curriculum units for youth and young people in The United Methodist Church.

Interest in the Millennial Generation: "[My interest] is twofold. First, these are the youth with whom I work in the local church and for whom I work in writing curriculum resources. Second, I teach a course on the Millennial Generation each January at Perkins School of Youth Ministry."

Article: "The Littleton Effect" (pages 111–13)

Susan H. Hay is director of Ministries With Youth, General Board of Discipleship, The United Methodist Church, Nashville, Tennessee. Susan is a contributing author for the "What Every Teacher Needs to Know About" series and has authored many articles and chapters in books.

Interest in the Millennial Generation: "Each generation has its mark it leaves not only on future generations but on existing generations as well. Ministry with the Millennial Generation draws us to new opportunities and challenges. This is a generation that has much to teach us adults—if we will but stop and listen to them."

Article: "Creating a Discipleship System for Youth and Young Adults" (pages 127–32)

Chris Hughes is director of Discipleship Ministries, Connectional Staff, Southeastern Jurisdiction, The United Methodist Church. He is coauthor (with Jennifer McSwain) of *The Kadasha Worship Workbook: Experiential Worship for the Next Generation* and coproducer of two videotape resources on postmodern worship and evangelism.

Interest in the Millennial Generation: "I am pursuing a lifelong commitment to ministry with youth and young adults. Gotta keep up!"

Article: "Youth and Their Music" (pages 83–88)

Jan R. Knight is editor of *Pockets* magazine, published by Upper Room Ministries, the General Board of Discipleship, The United Methodist Church, Nashville, Tennessee. She is coauthor (with Lynn Gilliam) of the book *My Journal: A Place to Write About God and Me.* She has written for *Interpreter, Pockets Newsletter, At Home With God,* and *Upper Room Disciplines.*

Interest in the Millennial Generation: "Members of the Millennial Generation are the current readers of *Pockets,* and will be for about ten more years. Aside from that, all of us need to be interested in each successive generation and how it will impact our world as we age and the world of our children and grandchildren."

Article: "Helping Children Find God" (pages 99–102)

Carol F. Krau is director of Christian Formation and Spiritual Leadership, the General Board of Discipleship, The United Methodist Church, Nashville, Tennessee. She is the author of *Keeping in Touch: Christian Formation and Teaching* and is a contributing author for the "What Every Teacher Needs to Know About" series and for the book *Staying Focused: Building Ministry Teams for Christian Formation.*

Interest in the Millennial Generation: "I am committed to assisting teachers and small-group leaders in creating settings in which members of the Millennial Generation can experience the presence of God and be formed as Christian disciples."

Article: "Reinventing the Sunday School" (pages 137–40)

Jasmine Miller, a sixth grader, was in the *Now Is the Time* video and has written for *Pockets* magazine.

Article: "The 411 on My Generation" (pages 77–78)

Julie O'Neal is in her final year at Saint Paul School of Theology in Kansas City, Missouri, to obtain her Master's of Theological Studies with an emphasis in Church Leadership. She works in the Admissions and Spiritual Formation/Field Education Offices at Saint Paul as a Lilly Intern. She has written for the magazines *The Upper Room* and *Devo'Zine* and contributed to the book *365 Meditations for Young Adults.*

Interest in the Millennial Generation: "[I am] interested in the way that the church is reaching out to those who are young adults, and this interest has carried through into looking at how the church is preparing those young people who are of the Millennial Generation."

Article: "Discerning God's Will" (pages 103–6)

Robert D. Pierson is senior pastor of Christ United Methodist Church, Tulsa, Oklahoma.

Interest in the Millennial Generation: "My interest in the Millennial Generation comes out of my great concern for the relevancy of the church to that younger part of our society. I am concerned about the future of the church in the next seventy-five years and how that will be worked out with this new Millennial population boom."

Article: "The Church as Family" (pages 63–68)

Victor Quon is the English-speaking pastor at West Valley Christian Alliance Church. He is executive director of the Malachi 4.6 Network (www.M46.org), a new ministry to train and teach youth workers in Asian churches for the Millennial Generation.

Interest in the Millennial Generation: "I am thrilled to observe the adventurous spirit of students in the Millennial Generation. I want to have some small role in seeing what God will do with these young men and women to bring revival and renewal in their nation and throughout the world."

Article: "Becoming Multiethnic" (pages 145–48)

James H. Ritchie, Jr. is a composer, freelance writer, teacher, and consultant in the areas of multigenerational ministries and human sexuality education. He wrote the curriculum *Created by God: About Human Sexuality for Older Boys and Girls;* edited and composed for the 2000 vacation Bible school, *Club Can-Do: Kids Called to Care;* and wrote for the curriculum *Exploring Faith: God's Word for God's Children.*

Interest in the Millennial Generation: "Given their very broad experiential base, Millennials are going to need help constructing a framework for conversations with their children—particularly those conversations where they will need to guide their children's decision-making process."

Article: "Dialogue for a Healthy Sexuality: The Church's Unique Opportunity" (pages 89–92)

Soozung Sa is director of Ministries With Families and Singles, the General Board of Discipleship, The United Methodist Church, Nashville, Tennessee. She is the author of the book *Caring From the Inside Out: How to Help Youth Show Compassion* ("SkillAbilities for Youth Ministries" series) and a contributor to the curriculum *Soul Tending: Life-Forming Practices for Older Youth and Young Adults.*

Interest in the Millennial Generation: "The Millennial Generation is not just the future but the present. It is quickly defining where our time, energy, and money go. We need to embrace this generation as significant leaders of today, not just of tomorrow, as they will continue to affect the patterns we set and the trends we follow."

Article: "Building Healthy Relationships" (pages 41–44)

Rob Weber is the founding pastor of Grace Community United Methodist Church in Shreveport, Louisiana. He is the author of the book *Visual Leadership: The Church Leader as Imagesmith* and of the book and video resource *Reconnecting: A Wesleyan Guide for the Renewal of Our Congregation.*

Interest in the Millennial Generation: "I have a large and growing number of Millennials in my congregation, one of whom is my son. These creative children are growing up with the tools of digital expression as much a part of their language as words and crayons. They will lead us into new ways of communicating the gospel to an increasingly digital world. I also believe that they will face some very difficult times during their lives and will receive strength from the church as well as being the leadership of the church as they grow."

Article: "The Pastor's Role With Millennials" (pages 149–52)

Kelly Welty is a high school student in New York who is one of many students who were asked to keep a diary of events at the turn of the millennium.

Article: "Dear Diary" (pages 71–76)

Kevin Witt is director of Camp and Retreat Ministries, the General Board of Discipleship, The United Methodist Church, Nashville, Tennessee. He is coauthor (with Marcey Balcomb) of the book *Twists of Faith: Ministry With Youth at the Turning Points of Their Lives* and the author of the online article "The Practice of Spiritual Leadership" (www.gbod.org/camping/articles.asp) and of numerous articles on faith formation, spiritual leadership, and camp/retreat ministry in religiously affiliated publications.

Interest in the Millennial Generation: "The Millennials can be quite committed to endeavors that have integrity and that make a real difference in the world. I believe there is great potential for supporting these young persons in developing and living as spiritual leaders who will lead the whole society. This generation must address huge issues with practicality, wisdom, and, most importantly, love. The Christian church has a very important role to play in being relevant and in inspiring spiritual leaders who lead the way of love."

Article: "The Power of Turning Points" (pages 107–10)

We thank Carolyn Poole, Deborah Carvin, and Carol Templeton for contacting writers and processing information from the Millennial Generation Survey.

A Beginning Point

Making God Real

Titles are tricky. We know you cannot make God real; that is under God's providence. But Christians are responsible for creating relationships and settings where people can encounter God in new ways. Rob Weber, pastor of the Grace Community Church in Shreveport, Louisiana, tells of what happened one Easter Sunday during children's time: Children were given an opportunity to decorate Easter eggs. One little boy, full of excitement, exclaimed for all to hear, "Easter makes God real!"

One of the greatest challenges for each Christian is to become a witness to God's presence in his or her life—to make God real. In Acts 22:15, Saul, who became the apostle Paul, received this word from Ananias: "You will be [God's] witness to all the world of what you have seen and heard."

God called Paul to be a witness, to make real for the people of his generation the love and salvation offered through Jesus Christ. Today, the greatest challenge facing the church is to be God's witness to our children and young people. The Millennial Generation is on the verge of a key moment in its life. By 2006, we will see a youth boom larger than any of the youth booms of the past. Fueled by the largest generation the world has ever seen, this youth boom will shape the values and trends for the next twenty years.

Purpose and Uses for This Book

In 1997, staff at the General Board of Discipleship of The United Methodist Church began a research project to listen to the needs and concerns of the Millennial Generation. Through a series of consultations, *Now Is the Time* seminars, and national surveys, we began to get a picture of this generation. It is this picture that we show in this book. This book offers ideas from several authors who share their insights about ministry with Millennials.

Before you begin to read, check the "Top 10 Ways to Use *Making God Real for a New Generation*" (page 5). We hope this list will spark your imagination as you read so that this material does not simply sit on a shelf.

Note also the "Study Guide" (pages 155–64). Use it with administrative groups in the church, teachers and leaders, parents, and Millennial Generation young people. It provides an overview of the materials in this book and will help you and your church consider the implications of issues related to the Millennial Generation.

What You Will Find as You Read

Section One: We begin with a section called "Who Are the Millennials?" Based on the U.S. Census, reports from the Department of Education, and the results from the 2002 Millennial Generation Survey of the General Board of Discipleship, these pages give a quick overview of some of the key characteristics and issues facing the Millennial Generation.

Sections Two through Five focus on how congregations and families can be witnesses for this Millennial Generation. We chose these sections because research supported the importance of the major categories of family, the world, spirituality, and ministry.

Section Two: "Millennials and Their Families" focuses on the life cycle of Millennials and the impact families have on their values, beliefs, and futures. It addresses healthy relationships and extending the family through the congregation.

Section Three: "Millennials and Their World" looks at key issues Millennials face in their day-to-day living. Two personal accounts from Millennials add to our perspective of how they view life and the challenges of school, home, and church.

Section Four: "The Spirituality of Millennials" paints a picture of a generation that seeks God in many ways—perhaps not radically different from previous generations but in ways that challenge us to ask, "What are we doing to partner with young people in finding God?"

Section Five: "Models for Ministry With Millennials" suggests some key ways congregations can create opportunities to be in ministry with Millennials.

You will find quotations, charts, and graphs based on the 2002 Millennial Generation Survey. Conducted by the Center for Evangelism at the General Board of Discipleship in high schools across the United States in February 2002, this survey of five hundred Millennials highlights the common experiences and attitudes of this generation.

Selections from this survey are included for your information (pages 167–70).

Remember that the ideas offered in Sections Two through Five are not exhaustive. They are chosen to help the reader move from "What have I read?" to "What can I, as one who cares for young people, do—in the family, in the church, and in the community?"

Our Hope for You

We hope that *Making God Real for a New Generation: Ministry With Millennials Born From 1982 to 1999* will encourage you and your congregation to be a people though whom God will touch the lives of many Millennials in the name of Jesus Christ. We pray that your congregation will be blessed by the gifts and insights Millennials offer. Each generation brings its own voice to the table. Now is the time for the Millennials to teach us and for the church to be their guide along the way.

Craig Kennet Miller
and
MaryJane Pierce Norton

Section One

Who Are the Millennials?

We, just like every generation before us, do have our problems. Along with the problems, however, come abundant promises. We are not Generation X; we are Generation Excellent.

High school student
Millennial Generation Survey, 2002

We are the children of the 80's. There will be a second coming of yuppies, greed, and bad-hair bands. I can see it now!

High school student
Millennial Generation Survey, 2002

Who Are the Millennials?

Craig Kennet Miller

Today's children and young people make up America's largest generation, the Millennials. They are on their way to making a huge impact on the way we see and experience the world around us. Born from 1982 to 1999, the Millennials are larger in number than the Baby Boomers or the Postmoderns. In 2003, they range in age from four to twenty-one. As the first generation to reach maturity in the twenty-first century, Millennials will play a pivotal role in shaping the future.

00000--1982/1999--00000 Generations in 2003

GIs	1910–1927	Also known as Builders. Life-shaping events include the Depression and World World II. They are now age 76 to 93.
Pioneers	1928–1945	Also known as Silents. They have led social change in music and culture. Elvis, Little Richard, and the Beatles are from their generation. They are now age 58 to 75.
Baby Boomers	1946–1963	Led by the high school class of 1964, they were shaped by the events of the 1960's and 1970's. Bill Clinton and George W. Bush come from this generation. They are now age 40 to 57.
Postmoderns	1964–1981	Also known as GenXers. Born right after the assassination of President Kennedy, they are the first generation to live with a Postmodern perspective. They are now age 22 to 39.
Millennials	1982–1999	Our largest generation, they are led by the high school class of 2000. They will set the major trends of the next twenty years. They are now age 4 to 21.
Genomics	2000 +	They will be the first generation to see the benefits and perils of the coming genetic revolution. They are now age 3 and under.

Look around you to see the power of the Millennials:
- record school enrollment, with more than fifty-three million in K–12 in the 2001–2002 school year;[1]
- a sixteen-percent projected increase in college enrollment from 2001 to 2011;[2]
- record box-office hits for preteen movies, such as *Shrek, Spider Man, The Lord of the Rings,* and *Harry Potter;*
- increasing sales in the newest alternative music: Christian Rock;[3]
- the popularity of *Dora the Explorer,* whose main character speaks English and Spanish, becoming the most-watched TV show by preschoolers;[4]
- 16.2 percent who live in poverty, the highest rate for any age group.[5]

If these facts do not get your attention, think of this: In 2006, we will see the emergence of a new youth boom that is larger than the historic youth boom of the 1960's and 1970's. Like youth booms past, it will challenge the beliefs and attitudes of the previous generations and, in turn, help define the values of the next twenty years.

Youth Booms Past and Present

About every eighteen years, the United States experiences a youth boom, when its youngest generation reaches the ages of seven to twenty-four. This is a critical time in a generation because it is at this time that a generation finds its voice and is able to influence the whole culture. It is also during this time that a generation forms the beliefs and values that it carries with it as it transitions into adulthood. Look back and you will see the pattern of change as each generation has entered its youth boom.

1934–1940: The GIs

From 1934 to 1940, the GI Generation had its youth boom. If it had not been for World War II, this generation might have been called the Swing Generation because of its love for big band music and swing. Sandwiched between the Depression and WWII, this time was when comic books hit the scene, with characters such as Superman. A child actress, Shirley Temple, was the queen of the box office at the movies, and every girl wanted to have a doll patterned after her likeness.

Movies such as *Snow White, Gone With the Wind,* and *The Wizard of Oz* became classics as they broke new ground in technology. It was also a time of social unrest as young people lived through the results of a depression that seemed to block their dreams for the future. New government programs such as Social Security and the New Deal promised to get America back on the right footing. In Europe and Asia the specter of war with Germany and Japan was on the horizon.

1952–1958: The Pioneers

The Pioneer Generation experienced its youth boom from 1952 to 1958. During their youth boom, the Pioneers invented a new style of music, rock 'n' roll. With Elvis and Little Richard leading the way, young people danced to a new beat. Other Pioneers, such as the Beatles, the Rolling Stones, and the Supremes, kept this youth boom exploding throughout the sixties. Movies such as *Rebel Without a Cause* and *The Blackboard Jungle* cast light on a new teen culture that seemed dangerous and foreboding to parents.

The transistor radio freed the radio from the big box in the living room to become a portable communicator that could be heard under the bedcovers in the middle of the night. As TV became more accessible, it soon became the dominant form of entertainment in the home as comedians such as Bob Hope and shows such as *I Love Lucy* were beamed into households across America. During this time, Disneyland opened and introduced a new concept for children's entertainment, the theme park.

Inventions such as the H-bomb and Sputnik created a climate of suspicion as the Cold War with the Soviet Union had its beginnings. Young people in their early twenties found themselves fighting during the Korean War, the first American war that did not end in complete victory.

The battlefront for civil rights for blacks was fought in the schools of the Pioneer Generation. The Brown vs. the Board of Education ruling by the Supreme Court in 1954 outlawed segregation in the nation's schools. In 1957, a high school in Little Rock became the center of focus as white mobs fought against the admission of nine black students to the high school. Martin Luther King, Jr., a Pioneer who was born in 1929, became the voice of his generation as he lead the civil rights movement until his assassination in 1968.

The civil rights and anti-war movements of the 1960's were led by the activist members of the Pioneer Generation. From the countercultural movement to the feminist movement, the leading voices for change were Pioneers.

1970–1976: The Baby Boomers

While Baby Boomers experienced the unrest of the 1960's during their childhood and youth, it was not until 1970 to 1976 that the Baby Boomer Generation experienced its youth boom. (Remember, a youth boom hits when a generation is age seven to twenty-four.)

Commentators of the time, such as Tom Wolfe, point to the demise of the counterculture movement after Woodstock in 1969 and the breakup of the Beatles in 1971 as a point in which society made another culture shift. Wolfe proclaimed the decade of the 1970's as the Me Decade, a time when youth became introspective and sought for values in a wide variety of spiritual quests.

In the church, the youth boom was most clearly seen in the Jesus Movement that started when hippies became converted to Christianity in the early 1970's. On Broadway, twenty-three-year-old Andrew Lloyd Webber combined his talents with twenty-six-year-old Tim Rice to bring us *Jesus Christ Superstar,* which made the story of Jesus accessible to the Baby Boomer Generation.

Musicians such as The Jackson Five and the Osmonds introduced teenybopper music to their adoring fans. As the youth boom progressed, hard rock and disco dominated the music scene, with the movie *Saturday Night Fever* portraying life in the fast lane.

During the Baby Boomer youth boom, the Vietnam War protests reached their zenith with the ending of the war. The feminist movement and the Jesus Movement both challenged the conventions of society. While feminists challenged the notion of a male-dominated society, the Jesus Movement challenged the church to accept a new brand of music and new forms of worship.

Two young college dropouts, Bill Gates and Steven Jobs, competed and created two companies that reshaped the way we work and interact with one another. The two companies they formed, Microsoft and Apple Computer, led the technological breakthroughs that created the revolution that put a personal computer on the desktops and in the briefcases of the world's workers.

1988–1994: The Postmoderns

The Postmodern Generation, also known as Generation X, had its youth boom from 1988 to 1994. Even though this generation was smaller in number than the Baby Boomers, the Postmoderns still had an impact on the larger culture. Grunge music and rap challenged society to pay attention to life on the edges. Alternative music gave women artists such as Alanis Morissette and Jewel a leading voice for their generation. Selena, and later Ricky Martin, became crossover artists who made Latin music popular for the whole generation.

Children of the Postmodern Generation were introduced to a whole new set of Disney characters. Preteens and children filled movie houses to watch Disney's series of new animated films, including *The Little Mermaid* and *Beauty and the Beast*. *The Breakfast Club* portrayed youth looking for meaning in their life, while *Ferris Bueller's Day Off* portrayed a generation that was a little bit more savvy than the older generations gave them credit for.

During its youth boom, the Postmodern Generation saw the end of the Cold War with the collapse of the Soviet Union and found itself fighting in the Persian Gulf War. Postmoderns were on the forefront of new technological breakthroughs, such as the Internet. As the first generation to have more than thirty percent of its parents going through a divorce or separation, they longed for healthy relationships and learned the importance of being able to make it on your own. As Postmoderns challenged the beliefs of the modern age, postmodernism became a new way to view a world with questions about what is true and whose beliefs are the most important.

2006–2012: The Millennials

When the Millennial Generation reaches age seven to twenty-four in 2006, we will experience another youth boom. Like youth booms past, it will challenge the conventions and beliefs of older generations. This generation will create its own music and culture and, as new leaders emerge, its voice will be heard.

This new youth boom will be shaped by seven key characteristics: The Numbers Game, The Tiger Effect, The New Gender Gap, Art as Window on the World, The New Multiethnic Mix, There Might Not Be a Tomorrow, and Relationships Count. When put together, these characteristics will produce a generation with its own way of viewing and interacting with the world.

Seven Characteristics of the Millennial Generation

As congregations shape ministry for the Millennial Generation, there are seven characteristics to which they need to pay attention.

1. The Numbers Game

The first thing you need to know is that Millennials are larger in number than the Baby Boomers or the Postmoderns. While the overall age of the population will go up as the Baby Boomers move toward retirement, we must not lose sight of the continued growth in the numbers of those under eighteen years of age. The U.S. Census taken in 2000 gives us the most current and accurate count of the numbers of each generation. Note this analysis of that census information.

Generation	Date of Birth	Youth Boom	Age in 2003	Numbers in 2000
Millennials	1982–1999	2006–2012	4–21	76,345,410
Postmoderns	1964–1981	1988–1994	22–39	72,010,866
Baby Boomers	1946–1963	1970–1976	40–57	73,799,193
Pioneers	1928–1945	1952–1958	58–75	39,263,369
GIs	1910–1927	1934–1940	76–93	18,881,203
WWI	1892–1909	1916–1922	94 and up	1,121,865

Schools Feeling the Impact

The nation's school systems have been the first to feel the impact of these larger numbers. During the 1987–1988 school year, attendance in K–12 was 45,487,000. By 2005–2006, attendance will peak with a 15 percent increase to 53,397,000.[6] Record numbers of students will continue to enroll in our nation's schools, and today's numbers are even higher than those during the heyday of the Baby Boomers in the 1960's and 1970's. By 2100, the number of new students will increase by 42,000,000, bringing the total to 94,000,000 school-age children.[7]

A landmark report by the U.S. Department of Education in 2000[8] details the challenges presented by these growing numbers of students:

- We will need an estimated 2.2 million new public school teachers in the next decade.
- We will need to spend an estimated 127 billion dollars to renovate and modernize schools.
- One-third of schools will use portable classrooms.
- Seventy-eight percent of all schools in rural America need to be repaired.

School districts in the South and the West are feeling the pangs of growth. The Los Angeles Unified School System projects a shortfall of 85,900 desks by 2005. In 2000, school officials said they needed to build 100 new schools in the next ten years and hire 4,000 additional teachers each year. In Miami the school system has to build one elementary school a month to keep up with the influx of new residents. Las Vegas is expected to see an increase of 150,000 students by 2010, which means a need for 88 new schools and 1,200 new teachers.[9]

Colleges Are Next in Line

From 2001 to 2011, there will be a 16-percent increase in the number of students on the nation's college campuses. Because this growth will come from the enrollment of the Millennials, there will be more students attending on a full-time, rather than on a part-time, basis. As a result, full-time enrollment is projected to increase by 19 percent from 2001 to 2011.[10]

Today, a college degree is what a high school degree was to previous generations. Ninety-one percent of Millennials in high school say they plan to go to college after they graduate. The effect is far reaching because it means there is now much greater competition to get into the most prestigious universities and colleges. Harvard, Princeton, and Stanford all find themselves awash in applications.

Straight *A*'s are no longer enough to get into some university systems. Some public universities, such as the University of California, are able to keep the cream of the crop, while students who would have been accepted in earlier times are shut out. As a result, college-bound Millennials are under great pressure to make high grades in school in order to give them a chance to make it to the college of their choice.

Where do you plan to go after high school?

	Overall	Male	Female
College	91%	87%	95%
Military	4%	6%	2%
Full-time work	3%	5%	1%
Trade school	2%	2%	2%

Millennial Generation Survey, 2002

2. The Tiger Effect

One of the offshoots of the competition to get into college is the high expectation that adults and parents have for their children. While children in some poor rural and urban areas of our country need more resources and attention, the vast majority of Millennials live in a suburban context that pressures them to succeed.

Blame it on Tiger Woods, if you want; or more correctly, blame his father. When Tiger Woods was an infant, his father set out to achieve a challenging goal: to turn his son into the greatest golfer of all time. Starting before Tiger could walk, he worked with Tiger daily to teach him all the skills necessary to become a great golfer. Now in his mid-twenties, Tiger *is* the greatest golfer in the world and an icon coveted by advertisers and golf fanatics alike.

Now parents of three-year-olds look at their sons and daughters and ask, "What could he or she become if we started now?" So, across the land we see soccer for four-year-olds and football for five-year-olds.

In generations past, children learned baseball and football at eight, nine, and ten years of age. Today, top-performing ten-year-olds are on traveling soccer, hockey, baseball, and basketball teams that lead to national championships.

Top high school athletes are courted by top-selling shoe companies who are looking for the next Michael Jordan or Kobe Bryant. Rather than going through the rigors of college life, the best high school basketball players are drafted straight into the NBA. While top players sign contracts worth millions of dollars, even a second-round pick will earn 300,000 dollars or more in the first year.

When Kobe Bryant was drafted out of high school by the Lakers in the 1996 draft, he not only signed a multi-million-dollar deal with the Lakers but also signed a multi-million-dollar deal with Adidas, largely as a result of his relationship with a marketing agent with Adidas who had spotted Bryant's talent at an early age.[11]

This is not to say that all this is negative. Many children have fulfilling lives and are learning lessons that provide them with great opportunities in the future. But when it gets out of control, children and parents become stressed out. Throughout the week many children are shuffled between sports practices, dance lessons, and music lessons, each having its own performance standards for children to achieve. For many, this pressure leads to a competitive atmosphere that puts children in a no-win situation.

What can a church do about youth sports?

- Identify adults to be chaplains for their children's teams.
- Train the chaplains to be spiritual leaders for the families of the team members.
- Teach the chaplains ways to help families keep winning and losing in balance.

Team chaplains are especially effective for high-achieving, traveling teams that take whole weekends to compete against teams in other cities.

The Test Game

As the government has placed more emphasis on tests as a way to determine school and teacher performance, school-age children are put in a pressure cooker to succeed. After all, their teacher's job depends on it.

One school teacher tells how she was in charge of the statewide test for her school. Before the test, she had to interview each child to confirm each one's racial-ethnic background and family configuration. Teachers had to sign an agreement that they would not do anything to help the children cheat. When the tests came, they were kept under lock and key. Rather then being a tool to help children learn, the test became a focus of worry and concern for everyone in the school.

When my fifth grader took her statewide test, the classroom took three weeks off regular lessons to focus on preparing for the test. The principal announced that the teachers were to back off from homework during this period, and parents were encouraged to make sure their children had plenty of rest during the week of the test.

Unlike generations past, children today are measured, tested, and examined early in life by both parents and teachers to see if they measure up. Pity the poor child who gets *C's* and *B's,* likes to play with his or her toys, and would love to run around in the neighborhood with his or her dog.

Because of this new pressure to succeed, many child-hood specialists, concerned with higher curriculum demands, advocate delayed entrance of boys into kindergarten to allow them to catch up with girls developmentally. For, believe it or not, while many girls are thriving in this new environment, boys are not. Today, the average eleventh-grade boy writes with the ability of an eighth-grade girl.[12]

3. The New Gender Gap

Projected college admissions reveal another startling fact: The percentage of men on campus is spiraling downward. Before 1979, men made up the majority of students on campus. Since 1979, however, women have been in the majority. By 2000, men made up only 44 percent of undergraduate students. By 2010, the number of males is expected to decrease to 42 percent.

Among some ethnic minorities, the gap at college is much wider. Among blacks 63 percent are women while 37 percent are men. For Hispanics it is 57 percent women and 43 percent men. Among lower-income whites, 54 percent are women and 46 percent are men.

On many campuses the numbers are even more troubling. At the University of Georgia in Athens, men make up just 39 percent of the freshman class. At Dickinson College in Carlisle, Pennsylvania, recruiters had to work extra hard to move the freshman class up from 36 percent to 43 percent male. At Chicago's DePaul University, men make up 41 percent of the college population.[13]

While many men may choose to go into the workforce after high school, the reality is that college graduates still earn almost double the wages of those who do not attend.

Boys in Trouble?

While it has been popular in the past to point to the gender plight of girls, the reality is that boys are falling behind girls in many areas in numbers that are hard to ignore. Boys make up two-thirds of those called learning disabled and receive 70 percent of the *D's* and *F's* teachers give. They get into more trouble than girls do: 80 percent of high school dropouts, 90 percent of alcohol and drugs violations, and 80 percent of the crimes that end up in juvenile court.[14]

Books like *Real Boys: Rescuing Our Sons From the Myths of Boyhood,* by William Pollack, Ph.D. (Henry Holt and Company, 1999), and *The War Against Boys: How Misguided Feminism Is Harming Our Young Men,* by Christina Hoff Sommers (Simon & Schuster, 2000), argue that our culture has largely ignored the needs of boys. Assuming that they will get ahead on their own,

little has been done to take into account the different needs of boys. While girls have had their own day at work with their parents, boys have not had advocates who challenge educators to pay attention to the ways boys learn, work together, and socialize. Rather than having a one-size-fits-all mentality, both voices call for a new effort to help boys compete in a culture that increasingly demands educated, verbal, and creative workers.

On a recent drive through urban Baltimore, I was told that young men there face high unemployment. At one time, a high school educated man could find a job in the shipyards and manufacturing plants that lined the harbor. These jobs provided a middle-class income and status in the community. Today, almost all of those jobs have been exported overseas. As a result, young men without a college education find themselves with few options for making a legitimate living. Instead, the easiest option is to live a life selling and buying drugs. A drive through the heart of the city reveals thousands of young men in the street without a chance for a real job that gives hope for a secure financial future.

This scene is repeated in urban and rural towns where men who once had an opportunity to work in manufacturing find themselves at a dead end because of their lack of education. Today's undereducated young person faces great obstacles to finding work that gives dignity and stability.

Over the last twenty years, a great shift has taken place. While young women have been encouraged to succeed, young men have been left to their own devices. Now it is not unusual to have a girl who is the valedictorian and the captain of the soccer team, but boys who succeed at such a high level are few and far between.[15]

The issue is not intelligence; the problem is that boys are underachieving. While young women have role models in teachers and women's professional groups who see their task as mentoring girls, young men are finding their role models in sports stars with multi-million-dollar contracts and high-tech leaders like Bill Gates and Steven Jobs, who left college to create Microsoft and Apple Computer. While the culture rewards young women who achieve academically, young men are not rewarded.

Boys and Girls Spend Time Differently

One of the most revealing questions in the 2002 Millennial Generation Survey (see excerpts on pages 19–20) has to do with how high school students spend their free time. When asked "Which do you most often do when you have free time?" the males and females responded with different number-one answers. For high school boys, the top three answers were "play a video/computer game" (51 percent), "watch TV" (45 percent), and "listen to music" (37 percent). For high school girls, the top three answers were "connect with friends" (59 percent), "listen to music" (53 percent), and "watch TV" (46 percent).

What is even more interesting is the contrast between the two groups. While 51 percent of males answered "play video/computer games," only 9 percent of females did. While 59 percent of females answered "connect with friends," a mere 36 percent of males did. When it came to "reading a book," almost twice as many girls as boys choose this as an answer (21 percent versus 13 percent).

In another set of questions, students were asked, "Have you ever?" Again, the differences between males and females are worth noting.

While females were higher in "cheated on a test" and "drank to get drunk," males were far higher in "viewed porn on the Net," "gambled," and "tried illegal drugs."

Which do you most often do when you have free time?

	Male	Female
Connect with friends	36%	59%
Watch TV	45%	46%
Listen to music	37%	53%
Play sports	36%	22%
Play a video/computer game	51%	9%
Surf the Net	27%	22%
Watch a video or DVD	27%	20%
Listen to the radio	14%	26%
Play music	22%	17%
Read a book	13%	21%
Pray	11%	16%
Connect with family	6%	16%

Millennial Generation Survey, 2002

Have you ever?	Male 9th	Female 9th	Male 12th	Female 12th
Cheated on a test	60%	74%	74%	91%
Drank to get drunk	18%	31%	44%	55%
Viewed porn on the Net	33%	7%	66%	17%
Gambled	26%	18%	57%	15%
Tried illegal drugs	7%	9%	31%	15%
Smoked pot	9%	13%	36%	33%
Regularly smoked cigarettes	15%	13%	28%	20%

Millennial Generation Survey, 2002

One more set of questions fills in the picture. When asked "Are you involved in one or more of the following activities?" answers from males were higher in "organized sports" and "work part-time," while females' answers were higher in "the arts," "religious youth group," and "service organization or club at school."

While it easy to say that boys are a problem to be corrected, another approach is to ask, "What is it that young men and women need to grow into healthy, mature adults?" After all, when it comes to the high school experience, a big change happens as youth move from ninth to twelfth grade.

Are you involved in one or more of the following activities?

	Male 9th	Female 9th	Male 12th	Female 12th
The arts	41%	64%	54%	57%
Organized sports	74%	52%	40%	32%
Religious youth group	44%	73%	39%	31%
Work part-time	22%	15%	65%	69%
Service organization or club at school	24%	40%	39%	52%
Youth organizations	20%	19%	18%	21%

Millennial Generation Survey, 2002

High School Experiences

A look at the involvement questions and the "have you ever" questions reveals another key point. As Millennials go through high school, they experiment with drugs, alcohol, smoking, gambling, and porn.

What is revealing is some of the contrasts between the males and females. Twelfth-grade girls scored higher in cheating on a test and drinking to get drunk, while their male contemporaries scored higher in viewing porn on the Net, gambling, trying illegal drugs, smoking pot, and smoking cigarettes.

When looking at their involvement with various groups and activities as they move from ninth to twelfth grade, both males and females see a sizable increase in working part-time. The participation level in organized sports and religious youth groups declines for both males and females from ninth to twelfth grade.

This same trend is seen in worship attendance. (See the figures on this page.) While 64 percent of ninth-grade males and 57 percent of ninth-grade females report going to a religious service weekly, by the time they are in twelfth grade, these numbers decline to 43 percent for young men and 40 percent for young women.

Note that participation in the arts by both young males and females remains high (page 19). What is it about art that keeps their attention and interest while other choices drop off?

How often do you go to religious services?

	Male 9th	Female 9th	Male 12th	Female 12th
Weekly	64%	57%	43%	40%
Twice a month	8%	7%	3%	11%
Monthly	6%	6%	12%	9%
Yearly	11%	16%	21%	21%
Never	11%	14%	21%	19%

Millennial Generation Survey, 2002

4. Art as Window on the World

While the Postmodern Generation lived out of a philosophy that rejected the modern views of the mid-twentieth century, Millennials live in post-postmodern times. Rather than tearing down what was before, Millennials are creating a worldview that has experience at its center.

In an experience-based culture, choices and decisions are made according to what is true for the individual. Values are built on the results of life-shaping events and experiences that inform what is right and wrong, what is real and what is false.

For Millennials, life is art. True artists express themselves based on life experiences. Using the tools at hand, paint and canvas or a guitar and voice, the ultimate goal is self-expression that reveals a pure emotion. This expression has the power to change others because it invites them to experience life through the artist's point of view.

Truth, then, is filtered through life experience. Truth is found not in head knowledge but in heart language. Rather than asking if something is true or false, the more important issue for Millennials is whether it touches the soul: Does it cause me to see the world in a different way? Does it call for me to accept a different point of view? Does it challenge me to make a change? Is it real?

While moderns based their worldview on scientific analysis and Postmoderns based theirs on the idea that there is no truth, the artist says there is a deeper truth that runs through human experience. When Forest in the movie *Forest Gump* cries after the death of his girlfriend from AIDS, there is a truth that all can identify: The loss of a loved one moves us to unbearable grief. No explanation is needed; sometimes life sucks.

For Millennials, the window to the soul is through artistic expression. While adults may see video games, movies, the Internet, computers, and cell phones as new technological devices that provide a vast array of entertainment options, Millennials view these as ways to connect with others, to share ideas, and to express themselves.

Through the magic of digital technology, Millennials are learning to take pictures with digital cameras and then load them onto computers with software that can reshape the image, add different colors, get rid of blemishes, or combine them with other designs. They are downloading music from the Internet to create their own CDs with their favorite songs. They are taking snippets of their favorite movies off of DVDs to create their own movies with dialogue and scenes from different films.

Which of the following do you have in your home?

91% Computer   87% Cable TV   85% Internet access

Which of the following do you have in your bedroom?

85% Television   55% Cable or satellite TV   40% Computer   29% Internet access

Which of the following do you carry with you?

70% Cell phone   47% CD player   10% Pager

8% Palm Pilot   6% Game Boy   3% Personal alarm

(or similar device)   (or similar device)

Millennial Generation Survey, 2002

While publishing companies and movie houses are crying foul over copyright, young people see music and movies as part of a sea of artistic options from which they can draw to make sense of the world from their point of view. The endgame is not making sure the writer of the song gets paid; it is the ability of the listener to reconfigure the information in a way that allows the user to create his or her own art.

Millennials have learned from rap artists the power of taking snippets of music from other artists and combining them with their own voice. Rather than living in the world of the physical, most Millennials draw their beliefs from the vast array of electronic culture that is theirs for the taking. If you ask a fourth-grade boy if he wants to play football, he probably thinks you are asking him to play the latest version of *Madden NFL* on his video game machine.

Go to school and watch a third grader make a Power-Point presentation in which she uses a video of Martin Luther King, Jr's "I Have a Dream" speech combined with a picture of the landing on the moon, the audio track from *Shrek's* "I Am a Believer," and her own comments about the sixties. When she gets an *A,* do you ask her where she got the material?

What sounds like selfishness is something much different. Awash in images and sounds from a hundred or more channels on cable or satellite TV; fueled by extensive choices of DVDs and video cassettes; gifted with unlimited access to information on the Net; armed with computers a hundred times more powerful than the one that went to the moon, with the ability to stay in touch on a cell phone no matter where they are, and with video game consoles that let one be a spy, a racer, or an alien—Millennials are creating a worldview that few adults can imagine.

What resonates at the core of it is the freedom to communicate and to create. A fourteen-year-old in Calcutta, India or Boise, Idaho can create a website that anyone in the world can see. The one who creates the website does not need a publisher, an agent, or a marketing company. All he or she needs is a hard drive that is big enough to hold the information, access to the Internet, and a willingness to send the message to as many people as he or she wants. And if enough people like what they see, he or she will be known. Life is art.

5. The New Multiethnic Mix

Millennials make up the most diverse generation the United States has ever seen. Fueled by the increase in immigration, Millennials represent cultures and languages from around the globe.

Thirteen percent of Millennials in high school say that English is their second language. Fourteen percent say that both parents were born outside the United States, and six percent say that one parent was born outside the United States.

English is your	
Native language	87%
Second language	13%
Parents were born	
In U.S.A.	80%
Outside U.S.A.	14%
One born outside U.S.A.	6%
You were born	
In U.S.A.	91%
Outside U.S.A.	9%

Millennial Generation Survey, 2002

In the Millennial Generation Survey, high schoolers identified themselves in these racial-ethnic categories:

62%   Euro-American
15%   African American
12%   Hispanic/Latino American
6%   Asian American/Pacific Islander/Native Hawaiian
4%   Multiethnic
1%   Native American

Another picture of the diversity of this generation can be seen using data from the 2000 U.S. Census.[16]

	Under 18	55 and Over
White, not Hispanic	66%	81%
Black	13%	9%
Hispanic or Latino (of any race)	14%	6%
Other race	6%	2%
Asian/Pacific Islander	4%	3%
Two or more races	3%	1%
American Indian	1%	1%

(The numbers do not add up to 100 percent because Hispanics/Latinos identify themselves by different races.)

This contrast between the "Under 18" and "55 and Over" groups gives a revealing picture of the difference in diversity between the youngest members of our society and the oldest. As the century progresses, non-whites will make up the majority of the population.

What about your church? Does your church look more like the demographics of the "55 and Over" or the "Under 18"? If your community is shifting to a multiethnic mix, what does this mean for the future of your congregation?

A Multiethnic Culture

Unlike popular shows for adults, such as *Frasier* and *Friends,* programs for preteens show high diversity in their casts. *Lizzie McGuire, Famous Jett Jackson,* and *All That* show day-to-day interactions between preteens of different races. The Disney Channel premiers a new made-for-cable movie every month that routinely represents the multiethnic makeup of Millennials.

When Nickelodeon launched *Dora the Explorer* for two- to five-year-olds, they wondered if a show about a seven-year-old Latina who mixes English and Spanish would find an audience. To their surprise, Dora is a hit, with an estimated 1.2 million viewers each times it airs. Because of demand for merchandise, *Dora the Explorer* products can now be found in stores across the country.[17]

While the Millennial Generation as a whole is quite diverse, most Millennials interact on a daily basis with their own racial-ethnic group. Of the sixteen high schools that were surveyed, only one school, H.B. Plant in Tampa, Florida, closely mirrored the national picture. When asked what they have experienced, fifty-eight percent of those surveyed said they have had a close friend of another race.

Have a close friend of another race
85%   Multiethnic
61%   Asians/Pacific Islanders
59%   Euro-Americans
48%   Hispanics/Latinos
36%   African-Americans

Millennial Generation Survey, 2002

What are your favorite kinds of music? (pick 2)

Hispanic/Latino
46% Rap/Hip-Hop
44% Pop/Rock
33% Latin
23% Alternative
13% Classical

Asian
74% Rap/Hip-Hop
61% Pop/Rock
52% Soul/Rhythm & Blues
26% Alternative
26% Classical

African American
94% Rap/Hip-Hop
52% Soul/Rhythm & Blues
11% Pop/Rock
8% Contemporary Inspirational
5% Gospel

Euro-American
72% Pop/Rock
41% Rap/Hip-Hop
24% Alternative
23% Country
11% Classical

Multiethnic
60% Rap/Hip-Hop
50% Pop/Rock
35% Alternative
35% Soul/Rhythm & Blues
10% Latin
10% Classical

Millennial Generation Survey, 2002

Music as Cultural Definer

As in all youth cultures, music is a critical part of one's identity and is an indicator of one's values. A look at the music tastes of high school Millennials gives us another picture of how diverse this generation is.

While rap/hip-hop has high universal appeal across the races, Latin music is heard mainly among Hispanics/Latinos and country music is heard mainly by Euro-Americans. Conversely, African-American youth are tuned in almost exclusively to rap/hip-hop and soul/rhythm & blues. Classical music was chosen among Asians at 26 percent and Hispanic/Latinos at 13 percent and was in the top five for four of the groups.

While not all Millennials live in a multiethnic environment, those who do are creating a new culture. If the children on the playgrounds of your community represent multiple races, and if there is a multiethnic dating pattern among youth and young adults, then the Millennials in your community are creating a new culture that respects and affirms their differences in a way that brings them all together. Churches that reflect this emerging culture will be best positioned to be in effective ministry with the Millennials in their community.

6. There Might Not Be a Tomorrow

Since the 1992 L.A. riots, Millennials have been confronted with more images and experiences of violence than ever before. From the two-year saga of the O.J. Simpson trials, to the Oklahoma City bombing, to the series of school shootings that culminated in the shootings at Columbine High School, to the horror of 9/11, Millennials are faced with the reality that this day could be their last.

As one high schooler said about 9/11, "It has left a pit of despair in our everyday life. There will always be a tiny bit of terror in people's hearts as they progress in life."

While adults woke up to the reality of terrorism on 9/11, Millennials have been living with fear of terrorism in their schools since the first shootings began. The titles of articles in the May 3, 1999 edition of *U.S. News & World Report* that focused on the Columbine shootings should get our attention:
• Why Teens Kill
• Inside a Youth Culture of Violence
• Do You Know Where Your Kids Are?
• What Worried Students Can Do
• Once Bullied, Now Bullies—With Guns
• Metal Detectors Alone Can't Do the Job
• Paying the Price of Protection

Replace *teens* and *youth* with *terrorists,* and you could have a series of articles written in the aftermath of 9/11. In the aftermath of Columbine, schools across the nation have staged mock drills to teach students what to do if one of their classmates decides to bring a gun to school to blow them away. Instead of the nuclear bomb drills of the Baby Boomer Generation, today's children lock down their classrooms and practice the drop drill if someone opens fire in the school.

Violence is not something that happens out there; it is something that can happen in your classroom, in your home, or at the local store. This atmosphere of violence was compounded by the event of 9/11.

Which two are the greatest issues facing your generation?

41% Stopping drug and alcohol abuse
39% Stopping violence in schools and local communities
33% Fighting terrorism
28% Stopping racism and sexism
22% Taking care of the environment
20% Stopping the breakdown of the family
19% Fixing the education system
13% Fixing the economy

Millennial Generation Survey, 2002

How did the events of September 11, 2001 affect you personally? (pick two)

44% I have more respect for the military, firefighters, and police.
26% I am more aware of the future.
26% I am more patriotic.
22% I have a better appreciation of my family.
14% I am more religious.
14% I am afraid to fly on airplanes.
13% It has made no difference in my life.
11% I am more tolerant of people who are different than me.
7% I have more trust in our government.
6% I am more likely to vote in the future.
5% I am more likely to choose a career that helps other people.
4% I am less likely to live far away from home.
3% I am less tolerant of people who are different than me.

Millennial Generation Survey, 2002

Effects of 9/11/01

For Millennials, the terrorist attacks on 9/11 will always be remembered. Millions of Millennials watched the events unfold before their eyes on television screens in the nation's schools. As the planes struck the World Trade Center and the Pentagon, they asked when it would ever end.

Reminders of 9/11 are hard to ignore. Textbooks used in the classroom prominently display pictures of the World Trade Center. Movies filmed in New York before 9/11 will have a least one picture of the World Trade Center. Now films and books have their own marker of before and after built into them.

New Heroes

Before 9/11, heroes were found on football fields and on baseball diamonds. Heroes were seen in famous actors and actresses who stood up for their cause. Heroes were imagined as action figures like Batman or seen in music stars who overcame great obstacles to become famous. One of the biggest results of 9/11 is that Millennials have a new set of heroes. Forty-four percent of Millennials said that they now have more respect for the military, firefighters, and police.

As a result of this experience, Millennials have been forced to see that the world is a bigger place than they once thought. As one Millennial said, "I think that 9/11 is our generation's Pearl Harbor. I think it woke us up and helped us realize we are not untouchable. Bad things can happen to us, and we need to strive to do our best to make the world a great place."

Another common sentiment was expressed by one Millennial, "It makes you think about your life and that tomorrow is never promised."

As a result, Millennials are asking hard questions about the meaning of life. They wonder if their life has a purpose. Many are searching for spiritual answers that promise them a life beyond this world.

More importantly, Millennials have been forced to become aware that the world can be a dangerous place. They are aware that not all people believe as they do and that some would even like to destroy their way of life.

7. Relationships Count

As congregations look to create ministry for Millennials, one vital key is the creation of healthy, strong relationships with members of this generation. When asked which experience has had the most impact on their lives, twenty-four percent point to the death of someone close to them. Thirteen percent said having a great coach or teacher was the most significant. Twelve percent talked about going through their parents' divorce.

These results point to something that cannot be overlooked when talking about Millennials: Relationships are key. The technology used by this generation, from cell phones to the Internet to instant messaging (IM), has a critical element: They are used by Millennials to stay in touch with friends and family. Increasingly, cell phones are seen by Millennials as a lifeline to friends and family when they face danger or are alone. For Millennials, technology is for staying connected. What is most important to this generation, like earlier generations, are the people who love them and the people whom they love.

Now Is the Time

As parents, grandparents, and congregations live out their relationships with Millennials, these seven characteristics point to something even more fundamental: Millennials need adults who are willing to listen to them. During the generation gap of the 1960's, youth said, "Do not trust anyone over thirty." Today's generation gap is the opposite; adults are saying, "Do not trust anyone under thirty." The most radical thing an adult can do is intentionally listen to and learn from today's children and youth.

Right now Millennials are forming the beliefs and values that will last them a lifetime. Christians cannot afford to wait, for to wait is to watch on the sidelines as this generation grows up before our eyes. Now is the time to focus our energy and time on creating places where we can learn from the experiences of Millennials and be mentors to them as they head into their youth boom. Now is the time to show our faith in Jesus Christ in ways that allow Millennials to know the grace and love of God that can transform them and in turn transform the whole world.

Critical Questions for Congregations

Congregations that desire to be in ministry with Millennials need to pay attention to four critical questions:

1. *Does worship tap into the artistic worldview of Millennials?*

    More than having a screen and a video projector used, Millennials long for an experience of God. By tapping into the ancient practices of the church, congregations can introduce mystery and create space for the contemplation of God.

    Many contemporary worship services are geared toward Baby Boomers but do not effectively tap into this longing for ritual and faith that spans beyond the last few decades. Millennials respond to an eclectic range of music, prayer, silence, and the sacraments.

    More importantly, worship that puts Millennials into leadership will attract members of their generation. When Millennials see Scripture readers, musicians, and ushers of their own generation, they see worship as a place where they are welcome.

2. *Is the preaching real?*

    Millennials want to hear preaching that comes out of personal experience and relates to their lives. They want to see how the Bible helps them deal with the tough issues of life: divorce, suicide, drug use, and sexual abuse. More than that, they want to see how the Christian life can make a difference in their relationships with their family and friends.

3. *Does the congregation focus on discipleship?*

    Congregations that take seriously the training of children and youth in spiritual disciplines, such as prayer, having a daily devotion, and doing acts of mercy for those in need, are the ones that are equipping their children and youth for the future. Rather than an activity-based ministry, these congregations focus on developing children and youth into Christian leaders. Youth are interested in being part of congregations that give them the spiritual tools to witness to their own generation about the saving grace of Jesus Christ.

4. *Does the congregation welcome children and youth?*
    If children, youth, and young adults are not welcomed, they will not come. Being welcomed means finding people who are willing to form relationships with them, to listen to their needs, and to learn from their life experiences. Welcoming means a commitment to an ongoing conversation about God's work in their lives and in the world. It means laughing and crying as Millennials name their joys and sorrows. It means extending the grace and love of Jesus Christ to those who may look and act different from ourselves.

Endnotes

1 *United States Department of Education News;* August 16, 2001 (www.ed.gov/PressReleases/08-2001/08162001.html).

2 *United States Department of Education News;* August 16, 2001 (www.ed.gov/PressReleases/08-2001/08162001.html).

3 "The Glorious Rise of Christian Pop," by Lorraine Ali, in *Newsweek;* July 16, 2001.

4 Associated Press article, by David Bauder, July 2001.

5 *United States Department of Commerce News;* September 25, 2001 (www.census.gov/Press-Release/www/2001/cb01-158.html).

6 "Projections of Education Statistics to 2011," National Center for Education Statistics (nces.ed.gov/pubs2001/proj01/highlights.asp).

7 *Baby Boom Echo: Growing Pains,* U.S. Department of Education; August, 21, 2000 (www.ed.gov/pubs/bbecho00).

8 *Baby Boom Echo: Growing Pains,* U.S. Department of Education; August, 21, 2000 (www.ed.gov/pubs/bbecho00).

9 *Baby Boom Echo: Growing Pains,* U.S. Department of Education; August, 21, 2000 (www.ed.gov/pubs/bbecho00).

10 *United States Department of Education News;* August 16, 2001 (www.ed.gov/PressReleases/08-2001/08162001.html).

11 *Sole Influence: Basketball, Corporate Greed, and the Corruption of America's Youth,* by Dan Wetzel and Don Yaeger (New York: Warner Books, Inc., 2000), pages 1–3.

12 "Are Boys the Weaker Sex?" by Anna Mulrine, in *U.S. News & World Report;* July 30, 2001.

13 "The Male Minority," by Daren Fonda, in *Time;* December 11, 2000.

14 "Are Boys the Weaker Sex?" by Anna Mulrine, in *U.S. News & World Report;* July 30, 2001.

15 "Are Boys the Weaker Sex?" by Anna Mulrine, in *U.S. News & World Report;* July 30, 2001.

16 "Table 1. Total Population by Age, Race, and Hispanic or Latino Origin for the United States: 2000," U.S. Census Bureau (www.census.gov/population/cen2000/phc-t9/tab01.pdf).

17 Associated Press article, by David Bauder, July 2001.

Section Two

Millennials and Their Families

Adults need to know how important we are and how much potential we have; they need to stop and listen because we have so much on our minds and so much to say about it.

High school student
Millennial Generation Survey, 2002

What Families Look Like Today

MaryJane Pierce Norton

00000—1982/1999—00000

If you were asked to draw a picture of your family, what would you draw? Would you include those who live in your household, or those who are part of your extended family, including grandparents, aunts, uncles, and cousins? Would your family be a group of friends not related by kinship but related by mutual care? Would your family consist of birth parents and foster parents? Would your family include siblings, half-siblings, and step-siblings?

America never really had one dominant family type. The families portrayed on such 1950's television shows as *Leave It to Beaver, Father Knows Best*, and *Ozzie and Harriet* may have been lifted up as prototypical, but even then the nation had a variety of family types. These television families may simply have been the least objectionable types of families to portray on television. Many people grew up thinking that their family was not as it should be because it did not fit these media images.

Attempts have been made to describe the right family, sometimes based on the Bible and sometimes based on Christian tradition. However, it is important to remember that the Bible contains no single definition of family, and neither does the church. In fact, just as we base our belief in a God who has created and is always creating, we know that there is a dimension of family that is ever-changing and always becoming a new creation.

Today, our children, youth, and young adults know that there is not just one family type. When they look at their own families, at their friends' families, at the families in their neighborhood, they see a wide range of family types, all of whom may be healthy and caring. They know that whether a family is healthy or not is not dependent on its configuration.

While the combination of people who make up a family does not control whether a family is healthy or not, the configuration of various types of families does influence the needs of children, youth, and adults who live in those families. Different family types have different needs. We will not catalog all the family types and their needs, but let's look at some of the types we see in our congregations today.

Dual-Earner Families

Many children, youth, and young adults live as part of two-parent families with children. In the majority of these two-parent families, both adult partners work outside the home. The dual-earner family is often a necessity today, for the family may find itself among the poor if both partners do not work.

And yet, with both adults working, these families face other difficulties, such as managing housework or solving the work-family conflicts associated with two jobs. And with two work schedules, as well as school and family schedules, many families spend hours negotiating who will do what, with which family member, and when. Children and youth often find themselves managing alone in the home as adults work long hours and have little leisure time.

For dual-earner families with children, the biggest challenge is finding reliable, high-quality, affordable childcare. For many, a large portion of their working income goes for this basic necessity. For others, the children end up caring for themselves from the end of the school day until their parents arrive home, sometimes late in the day.

Stay-at-Home Parents

Almost one quarter of children under eighteen are being raised by a working parent and a stay-at-home parent. After decreasing for many years, this family type has grown in the last five years from thirty to thirty-five percent, especially among families with children under six years old. This group includes both stay-at-home moms and stay-at-home dads. Many of these parents take time off from their prior careers to spend time with their children while they are young. As the children move into school age and beyond, many parents return to careers outside the home.

Issues for these families include the financial challenge of going from a two-income lifestyle to a one-income lifestyle. Other issues revolve around loss of career progress and how to reenter the work force after taking time away. An additional concern surfaces around balance of time in the home and volunteer requests from schools, churches, and community organizations, since most of these organizations look at this family type as a source for easy volunteers.

Families of Divorce

Many children and youth live in households where parents have divorced. Once spouses divorce, there are inevitable strains on the family. Immediately following divorce, and sometimes even before the couple even plans to divorce, household routines and roles break down. As a single parent seeks to perform the tasks usually assumed by two adults, he or she experiences task overload. The children and youth may be called upon to take on more of an adult role in the working of the family. Or, in some cases, the adults will attempt to protect the children and youth, requiring even less of them than they might have required in a two-parent household. Either way, the family experiences stress because of the realignment of roles.

For many families, divorce causes an economic change. In the first year following divorce, the income of families headed by women decreases, sometimes by as much as thirty percent of what it was prior to divorce. The issues of custody and child support may dominate conversations. Children and youth may find themselves moving to a new location, involving changes in schools, in friends, and in church attendance.

Single Adults and Single Parents

As we look at family types, we find many young adults living alone or with a friend. While these arrangements are an accepted reality of this stage of life, such living arrangements are often questioned as adults age. So, while a twenty-one-year-old may find acceptance and support for living alone, by the time he or she approaches the mid-thirties, family, extended family, and friends may begin to ask questions about the young adult's life plans.

Because of the rising average age at the time of marriage and the frequency of divorce, men and women in America spend on average more than half their lives unmarried. The church can partner with singles to work for acceptance of a single lifestyle and to create a support network for those who are living alone.

Many of these single adults are single parents. Many of them are single parents as a result of divorce. However, a rising percentage of women who have never been married are birthing children and raising them with no identified father. These children may answer questions about who their father is in a matter-of-fact way, or they may become uncertain and embarrassed. Whatever the feelings, never-married parents raising children alone often share some of the same difficulties faced by divorced parents.

Gay and Lesbian Families

Many children and youth are growing up in families with gay mothers or fathers. For most, the children have been born out of earlier heterosexual relationships. In addition, many women have borne children through sperm donation, and others—both men and women—have won the right to adopt children. The issues facing these families may be similar to two-parent families: managing households, balancing work, and managing relationships within and beyond the nuclear family.

Remarried Families

An estimated fifteen million stepchildren under the age of eighteen live in the United States. And in nearly half the marriages now being contracted, at least one of the partners has been previously married.

The issues facing remarried families need to be understood in the light of a loss of a primary relationship. Whether by death, divorce, or no marriage, someone who was once a part of the household is out. Someone who was not part of that original household is in. All parties in the household have to rework relationships, language, household rules, and parenting patterns.

When talking with remarried families, it is not uncommon to hear complaints about complications because of visitation rules and parenting styles. For noncustodial families, there may be important issues related to bonding. A child or youth may spend little time in the new household and may always feel like—and perhaps be perceived as—a visitor instead of a family member.

Issues for remarried families also include finances. Child support may be provided, but the question of who handles the extra expenses

Millennial Voices

My mom and dad divorced when I was two. I never remember them living together. However, it was one of my childhood dreams for them to get back together, even though both had married. It never happened.

Chris, age 23

31

of braces, music lessons, sports uniforms, and camp are often sources of contention. For congregations, simply knowing which children and youth go with which family can be confusing. And sorting out times for events and projects among children and youth who go between one household and another can be daunting for children's teachers and youth leaders.

Children Raised by Family Members

A growing number of children and youth are being raised by their grandparents or by other family members. Grandparent-headed households are in every socioeconomic and ethnic group. In many grandparent-headed households, no parent is present. Thus, the grandparent (or other related caregiver) carries all the legal, medical, and financial responsibilities for the child or children. For many of these caregivers, important issues include finances, lack of energy because of age, feeling the need to take the place of parents but not feeling able to do so, and custody and child support. Common questions they have are about how to get financial assistance, healthcare and insurance, quality childcare, and counseling.

Ways to Offer Support to Families

With all these family forms and the challenges presented, each family has a basic need to know that they are not alone. The church can be there to support, nurture, and care for every family type.

As we look at support for children, youth, and adults, it is important to acknowledge the partnership of home and congregation. Consider these ways to help support families today:

- Watch your language. Show respect for the families, no matter the type, of all children, youth, and young adults with whom you minister.
- Show successful families of varying types in the illustrations used in newsletters, in worship bulletins, in Sunday school lessons, and in sermons.
- When you include families in worship services, reflect the variety in your congregation. For instance, in lighting the Advent wreath, include singles, grandparents with grandchildren, and foster families.
- Set before the congregation examples of what makes for healthy families of any type. Make sure that the members of your congregation know that healthy families are not violent, not abusive, show love appropriately, and include care for the basic needs of food, shelter, and clothing.
- Set up parent support groups that are related to both their personal needs and the needs for parenting particular age groups of children, youth, and young adults.
- Provide good referral information on such issues as time management, financial management, and alcohol and drug recovery.

What Your Church Can Do

Profile the families in a particular Sunday school class or youth group. Ask each child or youth to write a one-page description of her or his family. Get permission to display these on a bulletin board at the church.

Pointers for Parents

Help your child or youth have pride in his or her family. Schedule once-a-month family talks. When you gather, talk together about one person in your immediate or extended family. Ask everyone to contribute one idea of what is unique and good about that family member. Pray together for that person.

Growing Through the Life Span

MaryJane Pierce Norton

A story that has always fascinated me is the Simeon/Anna story in Luke 2:22-38. Both have watched and waited for a savior. When they see the child Jesus, they express praise to God for their hope of Jesus as savior. That story speaks to me each time I see a newborn. Although not anticipating a savior like Jesus, I do look with hope at each newborn, wondering how her or his life will unfold. I look at the child and hope for the unfolding of the child's life in ways that will help him or her grow in strength and in wisdom, just as Jesus grew.

Growth in many ways is a mystery. When we look into the face of a baby, we do not know if this child will face life with optimism or look for worries in every event. We do not know if this child will excel in art or music or science. We do not know if this child will mature in a hoped for way or meet with an accident or disaster that will shorten his or her life.

However, in the midst of all we *do not* know, we *do* know something about the expected growth through the life span. We do know about the expected needs at different ages. We do know of concerns that are common for people at different ages. These things that we do know help us understand our children and youth. This knowledge becomes crucial in the family and in the congregation. The more we understand about the various ages, the more we are able to live successfully as families and minister to one another in congregations.

Growth and development is influenced by at least three components:

- *Cohort Happenings*—This component is generational theory. Craig Miller tells about the Millennial Generation in the Introduction to this book (pages 13–26). Things will happen in our culture that will affect each of us. Cultural events that happen as we grow into adulthood help shape our outlook on life, our value system, and our behaviors. We do not yet know what all of the influences will be on this generation. Certainly, we do know that the disaster of 9/11 (September 11, 2001) is one of those influences. Undoubtedly, there will be others as this generation moves toward adulthood.

- *Normative Development*—Normative development is the expected development of humans. This component includes what we know about brain development that occurs normatively over time. It also includes the work of major theorists who have looked at how human beings grow and develop. Because it is based on a majority concept, not all expected development happens at the same time with all people. However, there is enough clustering that it helps us know what to expect most of the time.

- *Non-Normative Events*—These are specific events that influence the growth of an individual. They include deaths, accidents, divorce, and debilitating illnesses. These events cannot be predicted, but they often, at least temporarily, halt normative processes.

In this article, we will examine normative development. In every age grouping there will be learning from

- *Psychosocial Development*—The primary theorist here is Erik Erikson. While the tasks he identified do not necessarily correspond with the actual ages he named at the time he wrote, the tasks at various ages have held true.
- *Cognitive Development*—The originator of theory in cognitive development we use today is Jean Piaget. The new developments in brain theory have again expanded our knowledge. The theory of how we think still holds true, but it is much more complex than Piaget might have imagined.
- *Social-Learning Development*—B.F. Skinner contributed greatly to our knowledge of human beings when he documented the fact that behavior can be changed through a system of rewards or punishments.
- *Moral Development*—First developed by Lawrence Kohlberg, and then modified by Carol Gilligan, the theory of moral development has helped identify the way humans make moral decisions. Furthermore, it has helped identify what makes human beings at different ages decide what is right and what is wrong.
- *Faith Development.* One of the biggest learnings from the faith development theorists is that faith is full and complete at every stage of life. However, faith as faith seeking understanding and the building of knowledge is linked to the human capacity for thinking and reasoning. John Westerhoff has helped identify the relational aspect of faith: how we grow as we feel the sense of belonging, inclusion, and support. James Fowler's work has helped us identify the ways we think and reason as this connects to faith seeking understanding.

As we grow at every age, the normative influences are many. The summary of each age included here provides an overview of what we can expect at various ages, what the needs are at various ages, and how we can support growth at various ages.

Infants, Toddlers, and Three-Year-Olds

At one time, much of popular thought pointed to infants simply eating, sleeping, and eating some more in order to grow physically. People assumed that they did not need much else for their growth. What we now know is that the brain is capable of much more than has been recognized in the past. From birth, the infant brain receives impressions, makes connections, and grows. From birth, interactions with caring adults influence the development of the child's brain. Neurons develop at a rapid rate, and early stimulation increases this growth. Brain development is constant and rapid during the first three years.

Children in this youngest age group are sensory learners. They taste, smell, pull, and push to learn. Sounds attract their attention, and the combination of sound in music or words with movement aids growth.

DemoFacts

A twelve-month-old uses an average of three words. By age three, the child uses nearly nine hundred words.

Newsweek Special Edition: Your Child From Birth to Three, Spring/Summer 1997, page 39.

Children in this age group are by necessity dependent on adults to feed, clothe, shelter, and transport them. As they begin to talk and walk, they need adults to set limits for safety, provide space for growth, and help them increase their abilities to care for themselves.

While children in this age group are curious about other children, they tend to treat others as one more object to explore, particularly during the first two years. From two to three years of age, they begin to play with other children, but adults are still their primary focus. They need from adults dependability, safe and loving care, and stimulation. Children who receive these things in their family are receiving a fair start in the world. Those with uncaring, abusive families are at a disadvantage from the beginning because the stimulation they are receiving may not lead to health at all.

For our youngest children, faith is

• placing trust in caring adults. The overriding concern is that their needs are cared for in a dependable way. The earliest images of God are based on the kinds of trusting, loving interactions they have with adults.

Ages Three to Six

The rapid growth that began in infancy continues during the preschool years. Preschool children are processing information all the time, leading to one of their primary characteristics: a short attention span. Few things hold their attention long because the world around them is full of new, exciting discoveries, and the preschool child is motivated to try them all.

A common memory for me is picking up one of my children from preschool and asking, "What did you do today?" The answer: "Play!" Play is the work of children. They try out new ideas, new roles, and new identities through play. They practice talking, walking, skipping, and jumping. They pretend to be grown up with homes and families. They paint their thoughts and feelings.

The logic of preschoolers is not an adult's logic. They draw conclusions based on appearances. If they see trees blowing in the wind, they are likely to think that trees make the wind blow. Their logic includes a mixture of fact and fantasy.

Preschool children are still dependent on their families for nurture and support. We know that children who suffer abuse do not view their family as a bad family. It is all they know, so the conclusions they draw about how love is expressed are based on hurt, pain, and betrayal.

Preschool children need adults who care for them and live out the values of honesty, love, support, and dependability. Children model their own behavior on the behaviors they see in adults.

Adults are still favored playmates and confidants, but at this age children begin to develop friendship patterns with their peers. By age four, they begin to realize the power of friendships. A common threat heard in preschool classrooms is, "If you don't play with me, I'm not going to invite you to my birthday party."

Preschool children need limits, boundaries, and consequences they can understand. I remember riding in a car with a parent who was bothered by the noises his four-year-old was making. He said to her, "If you don't stop, I'll make you walk home." This threat was unenforceable, since we were miles from their home. It taught the child nothing about expected behavior and real results.

As children grow, they become independent in more and more ways; so they need safe opportunities to make choices. Each time they are offered the time and space to make a choice, they increase in confidence and grow in independence.

For preschool children, faith is
- having a sense of belonging. Hear them as they speak of *my* room, *my* teacher, *my* school, and *my* church.
- talking with adults who care. They particularly crave one-on-one time, since in today's society they often become part of a group as early as the toddler years.
- knowing church manners. This description may seem strange, but remember the focus on appearances. Preschool children love knowing when to sit and when to stand in church. They love coming to the Communion rail and kneeling with *their* church.
- having a God whose image is formed by adults in their lives. God becomes like Mommy or Daddy. If the parent is loving and kind, caring and compassionate, this is fine. But if the parent is abusive, the child's image of God may take on those characteristics they experience.

Ages Six to Twelve

Between the ages of seven and ten, children experience less-rapid physical change than earlier in their lives. However, they are still excited by growth, so it is important to notice the ways they are growing and changing. The most observable sign of growth is permanent teeth. Can you recall how excited a child is when he or she begins losing teeth? It is an outward sign that he or she is growing. It is also at this age when you may hear more about half ages. For example, a child is likely to say she is seven and a half, not simply seven. It is important to be growing.

Children this age have a growing awareness of the sense of self apart from others. Elementary-age children are testing what they can do and who they are. Much of what they decide about who they are is based on what they can or cannot do, so it is linked to such achievements as playing the piano or playing soccer. Those who cannot achieve in those kinds of measurable ways because of physical disabilities may have a difficult time.

Children this age are still thinking concretely and reasoning by observation. They will look at the cross at church and think, *Jesus died on the cross.* They do not think about such abstract things as grace, redemption, or salvation. Although children may know the words and be able to define them, they still cannot think in these abstract ways.

Brain development is also not at the peak it was, particularly in the period from birth to three years. Now is a time for resting before the next surge of activity. The next growth spurt at about age ten or so will lead to the beginning of abilities to think abstractly.

Elementary age is a time of growing peer relationships. Friendships become important.

Rules are also important to these children. They use rules to determine what is right and what is wrong. They make moral decisions based on whether the rules say something is right or wrong.

Children this age need heroes and heroines: adults to look up to and emulate. They need these adults in their family and in their church and community. The more children interact with caring adults, the more they are able to find those models.

Elementary-age children see themselves as workers and want to produce something worthwhile. They want to be a part of serving in leadership at church. While they may not like chores, they like to contribute to things they see as important in the family, such as preparing a meal.

Much of the life of a child this age centers on school. Often, a child's self-image will derive from school: success in the classroom and success on the playground. Children who are labeled as discipline problems or who have learning disabilities need help from adults at home and in the congregation building self-esteem in spite of school.

For elementary-age children, faith is

- belonging. They wonder, *Am I welcome? Am I included?* This need goes beyond just having a place; it includes a sense of how the child is treated. *Do people speak to me? Do they know my name? Do they see what I can contribute?*
- knowing the rules. Elementary-age children learn and grow from knowing the rules of the church: the Ten Commandments, the Golden Rule, the story of Jesus telling us how often we need to forgive. The rules help them form understandings of what is right and what is wrong. They have serious questions when they see these rules being broken.
- being taught more (and not being left behind). Elementary-age children want to learn more and more. They may not want to recite, but they do want to know more about the God who claims them as children.
- being shown God's ways. Children are still dependent on adults to model God's love and care.

Ages Twelve to Eighteen

In our culture, adolescence is the bridge from childhood to adulthood. It may actually start as early as age ten; with the way we have pushed maturity downward, this can be the case.

The attitudes and commitments made in adolescence help shape the character of young adulthood. Adolescence is an important time in the journey of growth. It is also a time of rapid physical changes. Body parts do not always grow at the same pace, so children may have noses, ears, and feet that seem too big for their body. Many are embarrassed about the body that is growing in these odd ways.

This age is a time of gaining new cognitive skills, as children enter into another phase of rapid brain growth. With Piaget, we once thought that adolescence was when we arrived full-blown with the ability to do abstract thinking. However, we have learned from further study of brain development that this is the time of rapid development in that area, but it is just beginning and is not completed at this stage.

Adolescents are working at acquiring their own values: *My parents think church is important. My friends think it is boring. What do I think?*

While there is some debate about peer pressure in our society, there is no debate about the importance of peer culture. In his book *The Second Family: How Adolescent Power Is Challenging the American Family,* Ron Taffel calls this "the second family." His argument is that as adults who are always working, always busy, always on the run, we have left our youth to form family support with a second family: their peers. While they may not make decisions based on whether their peers will like them or not, they have help from their peers with the experience once they make a decision to experiment in sex or drugs or other behaviors. They behave as family.

For teens, moral reasoning goes beyond the question, "Will I get punished?" In fact, sometimes adolescents seem to make decisions in spite of consequences. Teens are risk takers, since exploring the dangers of the world excites them. They see themselves as indestructible, and they will take life-threatening risks without apparent thought to consequences.

For adolescents, self-absorption is taken to new heights: *my* hair, *my* clothes, *my* needs, *my* wants, *my* time schedule. And through all of this there is often uncertainty. James Fowler sums it up with this verse, "I see you seeing me; I see the me I think you see. But is that really me?"

Teens need a group to belong to. They wonder, *Which group am I in?* In some school settings, we can still see the delineation of jocks, scholars, nerds, cheerleaders, party-hearties. In other school settings, there is crossover in many of these groups. Group is important for adolescents.

Teens really do relish adults who will listen to them. They need forums for thinking and talking. Often, adults move directly into a telling mode with teenagers. However, it is important for adults to let adolescents state their opinions, try out ideas, and question what they see going on around them.

Family can be confusing for teens. They may be thinking, *I'm not just like them, but I still need them! Am I still a part of the family?*

For adolescents, faith is
- having God with them as a friend. At a time in life when adolescents may feel unsure about themselves, about their friends, and about their family, having God as a steadfast friend is important.
- taking comfort in what they know without appearing to do so. We sometimes call teens nonconformist conformists. Some have pierced eyebrows, tattoos on their ankles, and spiked hair, but they can still find comfort in the dependability of a familiar worship service.
- seeking and questioning. While not quite ready to declare where they find themselves, they need the space to ask questions and talk about doubts.

- telling about what they think they believe. Adolescents seek places to express what they feel and believe.
- exploring what is meant by call. This is the time when we begin talking with youth about calls to ministry, calls to service. While youth deal with other life issues, they also reflect on what their faith calls them to do and to be. This is also true in the world of school. I recently talked with a parent about colleges. She told me that by the time my child is a junior in high school, he will need to have some sense of what career he will be seeking in order to know which colleges to apply to. Call, vocation, and direction—all of these form part of the faith issues of youth.

Ages Eighteen to Thirty

While grouping broad age groups of children and youth together is daunting, it is even more so with young adults. Think about the many faces of young adults in your congregation and in your community. This group includes young singles without children, young singles with children, young marrieds without children, young marrieds with children, divorced singles; diverse lifestyles and sexual preferences; high school dropouts, high school graduates, college attendees, college graduates. It includes young adults who are unemployed; employed in work they see as simply work, not as a career; and professionals. Incomes range from poverty level to six- and seven-figure salaries. Some still live at home with parents; some are living by themselves or with friends; some are married with families.

People reach their physical peak during young adulthood. They keep improving and growing physically if they practice good nutrition and regular exercise. It is a time when physically many can do whatever they set their minds to do. The most recent brain research points to growth cycles at ages twenty and twenty-five. At these times, increased specialization and thinking occurs.

Young adults have established learning preferences. Some will say, "I hate working in small groups. Let me do this on my own." Others will say, "Let me be part of a group. I know we can do it together."

Young adults are finding their place in the adult world. Many are forming relationships that will last over time. Some are starting careers or jobs; others are establishing homes or preparing with that in mind.

Young adults need the ability to make their own choices about career, relationships, and vocation. They still need the help of community and family—sometimes for listening and reflecting, sometimes for testing—but the decisions are theirs.

Young adults are concerned with finances. For some, it is simply the finances of survival. For others, it is the finances of getting an education or establishing themselves in a vocation. Many become at-risk because of poor decisions about credit and credit spending. These problems can take years to correct, and young adults find themselves saddled with debt without anything to show for it.

Practicing intimacy in longer-term relationships is a task of young adults. These relationships may occur in marriage, in having children, in cohabiting with another.

Pointers for Parents

In all of development, interactions are key. It is not quality versus quantity; it is the nature of the interactions.

Rate yourself. How much time do you hang out with your kids with nothing planned except to be with them?

Kids say routines with parents are better than big events. What can you do?
- Attend a movie.
- Take a walk.
- Linger over a meal.
- Start a once-a-week game night.
- Make car rides talk time.

During young adulthood, people begin to struggle with the balance of friends/family and play/work and learning. A question for many becomes, Where does church fit in, or does it?

For some living on the edge, the young-adult years become a time of coping and surviving. Life offers little hope, and all energy is taken with day-to-day sustenance.

Young adults seek acceptance. It can be from other adults in their families and communities whose opinions they honor, from work situations, or from peers.

For young adults, faith is

- deciding how they see God today, as their view may change tomorrow. Young adults like small groups with whom they can be real and explore faith issues.
- questioning and experimenting. During the young-adult years, many try different faiths or faith expressions. For instance, while seeing themselves as Christian, they may practice forms of Eastern meditation.
- belonging. Young adults need a genuine, supportive community.
- serving. Again, young adults may explore different ways of serving. Today, they might choose short-term missionary trips, volunteer experiences in the community, mentoring with young people. However, by the next month or next year, they may have found another avenue of service to try.
- leading. Young adults enjoy leading as they grow.

Through all of these stages of growth, we seek to understand one another, to communicate with one another, and to grow together in faith. If we pay attention to the concerns, needs, and expected growth of others, we have a better chance of understanding their behaviors, their questions, and their strengths.

What Your Church Can Do

- Where can our young people live out their faith in ways that test their abilities and challenge their growth?

- In our congregation, where can our children and young people gather to talk about their faith and be listened to by adults?

- What do we provide for parents as support and learning in helping their young people form faith?

Building Healthy Relationships

Soozung Sa

If you wanted to build a perfect house that would last forever, so to speak, in the perfect setting, with no financial constraints, with everything you always wanted, how would you begin the process so that the house would meet all your needs? What would be some of the most important decisions you would need to make as you design this perfect house? Remember, this is the perfect house you have always dreamed of, so you would not have to make any compromises. Everything goes your way all the time.

If you wanted to build a perfect relationship that would last forever, so to speak, in the perfect setting, with no financial constraints, with everything you always wanted, how would you begin the process so that the relationship would meet all your needs? What would be some of the most important decisions you would need to make as you design this perfect relationship? Remember, this is the perfect relationship you have always dreamed of, so you would not have to make any compromises. Everything goes your way all the time.

Most of us will never have the opportunity to build such a house; but if we were ever asked this open-ended question, each of us could certainly come up with a response. Most of us will never have the opportunity to build such a relationship; but if we were ever asked this open-ended question, each of us could certainly come up with a response.

Such perfect relationships do not exist, but people of all ages, especially the Millennials, can be encouraged to strive toward building healthy relationships by considering four steps: (1) excavating your past, (2) accepting your past, (3) celebrating your present, and (4) influencing your future. This process for building healthy relationships must be modeled by their leaders and mentors. As Millennial children, youth, and young adults interact with you, they will notice traces of these steps in what you say and do.

It is difficult to compete with all the images that are out there shaping our young people. The world is moving much faster than we can even imagine. If our focus is on countering these images, we will be building on sand. Instead, we need to acknowledge these obstacles and then move onward. What the Millennials need is a chance to talk and to be listened to. They need people in their lives who will listen to their souls so that they can develop healthy selves and navigate through their own complex interior landscapes. Most young people are afraid of being judged by peers and adults, but they yearn to be listened to. They want to know how to juggle the complexity of life and understand the gray areas.

Pointers for Parents

People of all ages, especially Millennials, can be encouraged to strive toward building healthy relationships by considering four steps:
1. Excavating your past
2. Accepting your past
3. Celebrating your present
4. Influencing your future

Marty said to his youth pastor, "I kinda feel embarrassed to ask, but I have to talk about something. I know you will kinda be strict but serious about it because you know me, and my friends will come up blank or be immature about it."

Four Steps for Building Healthy Relationships

Step One: Excavating Your Past

Although one may examine the past all through one's life, it is not typically an exercise most people engage in with enthusiasm. Older Millennials can be encouraged to explore the patterns of their past by keeping a journal of thoughts on people (deceased or living) who have influenced them and whom they have influenced. They can be encouraged to write about people they are attracted to and admire from a distance. It will be helpful if they write why they think they admire or are attracted to certain people. They can keep a list of the relationships, marriages, or friendships they admire. Encourage them to write why they think they admire these interactions.

Younger Millennials can also keep a journal, but they may want to draw in their journals. (Of course, some of the older Millennials may choose to draw as well.) As these younger Millennials name the people who have influenced them or whom they admire, leaders can help them verbalize why they chose the people they listed.

For the youngest Millennials, reading stories about relationships with family, with friends, and with pets will provide an opportunity for leaders to ask the children about their own personal lives. Leaders do not need to provide any answers or conclusions. Just allowing the time to explore and reveal their past will help the Millennials begin the process of excavating their past.

Step Two: Accepting Your Past

Accepting is different from understanding. By accepting your past, you take charge of your life. You see that you have choices and emotions, and that you own them. They are yours. No one can take your feelings away, and no one can tell you how to feel. You can see that blaming people in your past relationships will only make you bitter in your current and future relationships. If it does not make you bitter, most likely you will repeat unhealthy patterns in relating to others.

Talking about your past in a public setting, such as a small group, can begin the process of accepting your past. (The small group should have no more than seven members, and an adult should be there to help facilitate the discussion.) Begin by passing out a piece of paper, the larger the better. Have each person draw a straight line horizontally across the entire width of the paper. Ask the group members to draw a little notch to the far left end of the line and write their birth year above the notch. Ask them to mark the far right end of the line with an arrow that continues to the right and then to write today's date above the arrow. If you have about forty-five minutes, have the group make about six notches along the line. (If you have less time, use fewer notches. If you have more time, use more notches.) You are now looking at a timeline. Ask each person in the group to think of people they have met and interacted with who have been significant in shaping them, either positively or negatively, as the person they are. Have the participants write the names of those who have influenced them under the line, aligned with the notches. Above the notches, have them put the year or years they think this relationship took shape. Making such a timeline will be a challenge, but encourage those making their time-lines to do the best they can to put the names in chronological order.

The name under the first notch, the birth year, should be a parent. Below the arrow at the end of the line (today's date) should be the name of someone who is now in their life as a significant friend or mentor. Give the group about ten minutes to complete the individual timelines, and then let them talk with one another about them. This opportunity to talk about their life may be the first time some in the group have looked at the people and events of their life in any linear way. By telling others about his or her life, each person can begin accepting it to a small degree.

Step Three: Celebrating Your Present

Celebrating the present may be the most difficult step for some. It is easy to dwell in the past, and we are often caught up in planning for the future. However, Millennials are communicating with others more than any other generation did when they were their age. They are able to send messages quickly and frequently through e-mail. Many of them have cell phones, so flagging them down is not as difficult as it used to be. In some ways, the Millennial Generation is more mindful of philanthropic endeavors than other generations have been. Such endeavors are a sign of living in the present. However, many Millennials still need help learning to make a deeper, more meaningful connection with others.

Although it may seem as though the Millennials are living in the present and for today, they need guidance and help in celebrating their present and making it more meaningful. They certainly do not want to hear about how good they have it. They need to be affirmed for their ideas and need guidance as they sort out what they believe. And most of all, they need to see, as a journal of their lives, all the flaws on their body, on their face, and in their past.

An activity that will help Millennials embrace this celebration of the present is to send them on a meditation journey:

- Set up a few meditation stations, either inside your church or out-doors. Prepare about seven stations that will take about forty-five minutes. Some station ideas might include the following:
  — *Station One:* On the floor by a set of stairs going up, place a sign that says, "As you take each step up the stairs, think of peo-ple who have mentored you or influenced you to accept you for who you are."
  — *Station Two:* By another set of stairs going down, place a sign that says, "As you take each step down the stairs, think of those whom you have loved and influenced as you helped them love and accept themselves as they are."
  — *Station Three:* Place a set of footprints along a hallway. On a wall at the beginning of the footprints, place a sign that says, "Place your feet on the footprints and walk along in the footsteps of Jesus. As you walk, what thoughts are flowing through you?"
  — *Station Four:* Place on the soda machine a sign that says, "How is your life like a vending machine?"

DemoFacts

Millennials are communicating with others more than any other generation did when they were their age. However, many Millennials still need help learn-ing to make a deeper, more meaningful connection with others.

— *Station Five:* Put a basket filled with ribbons in a room where there is a post or a rope hanging down from the ceiling. Near the post or rope place a sign that says, "Take a ribbon from the basket and tie it around the post (or rope). As you tie it on, say a prayer for someone who needs God in his or her life. Tie as many ribbons on as you would like."

— *Station Six:* On a mirror in one of the restrooms or in the choir room, place a sign that says, "As you look in the mirror, notice all the fine lines, freckles, scars, pimples, moles, bumps, and flaws. Take this time to celebrate who you are today and to embrace all the flaws. Realize and accept that these flaws and marks are a journal of your life. You have made it through a lot. Say thank you to our Creator who made you."

— *Station Seven:* In the sanctuary or chapel, have paper, pencil, and masking tape available. Place a sign by the cross that says, "Here is where you get to leave your burdens and problems. Come as you are. It is free, and no problem is too big or too small. Write the things you need to give to God to take care of, and tape the list to the cross."

• Number the stations and make a map of their locations.
• Give each person a copy of the map, and encourage each one to go on the meditation journey alone or with a younger person who may need help reading or understanding the questions. Explain that they do not need to go to the stations in sequential order, but they should all end the journey at the last station.
• When everyone reaches the final station, encourage them to talk about what they did, said, or felt at each station.
• Close with a prayer that lifts up the notes on the cross.

Step Four: Influencing Your Future

By engaging in some of the above activities, children, youth, and young adults will experience making healthy connections in a safe environment. They can begin navigating more confidently in relationships so that they have healthier interactions with others, especially in their family. They will connect on a deeper and more meaningful level when they talk with others about what they find as they excavate and accept their past and as they reflect on how they celebrate their present. At this point, it is critical for each person to have an adult who is not his or her parent to help process such thoughts for the future.

Sometimes our desire to have healthy relationships outside the family starts with steps that exclude our family. Eventually, though, we can bring our new perspectives and ways of reacting back to the dinner table at home so that we can then go back out into the world and ultimately have the healthy relationships we yearn to have, both with our family and in the community. Being able to have healthier interactions at home will give Millennials the tools they need to build healthy relationships with others in all settings.

DemoFacts

Millennials will connect on a deeper and more meaningful level when they talk with others about what they find as they excavate and accept their past and as they reflect on how they celebrate their present. They will also develop an appetite for healthy interactions in the future.

A Family Crisis or Families in Crisis?

MaryJane Pierce Norton

It is interesting to read newspaper headlines. Since starting my job as Director of Family Ministries in 1996, I have watched articles come and go that emphasize "the American family in crisis." The topic of these articles is the dissolution of the American family. Usually, statements are made about divorce and single parents and children in childcare. While any of those conditions may create a family crisis within an individual family, I can find no hard evidence to support the claim that families in general have radically changed in the last twenty years. Families today are diverse and complex, which has always been the case in American society. Diversity and complexity do not, however, inherently create a crisis. What might be different today is the lack of extended family and community support that existed at other times in our nation's history. Part of what congregations must do to support families is to look at what we have in place to support and aid families when they experience a family crisis.

Consider this litany of ills that can create stress in the family and a crisis for one or more individuals in the household:

- natural disasters, such as floods, hurricanes, fires, tornados;
- death of a family member, including grandparents or other extended family who may or may not live in the household;
- suicide of a friend or family member;
- illness;
- chronic disease, such as diabetes;
- mental illness;
- substance abuse;
- pregnancy of a teen;
- divorce;
- abuse;
- violence in the school or community;
- loss of job/long-term unemployment;
- loss of childcare;
- changing households, such as grandparents moving into the home or families with children moving in with grandparents.

Perhaps we do not need to pay attention to a broad statement of the family in crisis. Instead, we may need to pay attention to what gives an individual family the assets they need to live through and strengthen one another in the midst of family crises. After all, many crises can be weathered if families have the resources within themselves or if they are pointed to resources within the congregation or community where they can receive support.

DemoFacts

What have you experienced?

78%	Having a great coach or teacher
71%	Being on a winning team
61%	Baptism/Confirmation
55%	Having a close friend of another race
55%	Death of a grandparent
50%	A religious experience
30%	Losing your virginity
29%	Death of a close friend
24%	Your parents' divorce
21%	Counseling or therapy
20%	Parent losing a job
19%	A parent's wedding
15%	A parent's serious illness
10%	Addiction to drugs or alcohol
10%	Your own suicide attempt
7%	Physical or sexual abuse
5%	Death of a parent or a brother/sister
5%	Victim of a violent crime
3%	Having a baby

Millennial Generation Survey, 2002

This look at some things that create family stress and crisis is not comprehensive. Rather, it is illustrative of some of the things congregations can address as they reach out to the families of Millennial Generation children and youth.

Economic Concerns

One big concern for families during a crisis is the family's economic situation. In looking at the effect of different issues on the lives of children, the National Survey of America's Families noted a marked difference between children living in low-income households with those living in higher-income households. As we look at other problems families encounter, it is important to keep this economic factor in mind. When families live close to the economic edge, everything else becomes subject to their financial reality.

In households where there is economic uncertainty, this uncertainty alone creates a crisis. The stress is even greater if the family has additional worries, such as a family member with an ongoing physical condition or a family member with an addiction. Families that are economically healthy will not necessarily deal any better with another kind of crisis in the family, but they will not have to expend as much of their energy simply meeting daily expenses.

In relation to brain development, we know that children in low-income households may not receive the kind of stimulation they need for the best growth. In research regarding children and youth today done by the General Board of Discipleship, we find that there is an ever-increasing division between families that can provide economic stability and those that cannot. Because of this reality, we have to pay attention to economic health.

It is hard to ask families in a congregation, "How is your financial health?" But the answer to this question is key to ascertaining the needs of families. A congregation that can provide an atmosphere in which families can admit to needing aid is more likely to aid in the development of the individuals in a household. Congregations can provide information about applying for state and federal aid, establish a congregational help program for families in financial crisis, provide community and congregational classes on financial planning, and try to provide lower-cost options in all programming. A friend recently told of an experience of pairing a youth program where the families had low incomes with another congregation where the families had middle to high incomes. She reminded me that what one might take for granted for one group, such as sleeping bags for camping out, can be nearly impossible for another group.

Chronic Illness

Illness does not ask; it demands. As a result, the energy of a family often gets sucked into an illness so that the illness is the center for all of family life. When this happens, a series of stressors for the family, in addition to the illness itself, are created.

Consider the viewpoint of the child if a parent is chronically ill. Many children adapt their behavior to the needs of the parent, becoming

DemoFacts

- In 1999, thirteen percent of children and adolescents were overweight.

- One-fourth of children in America spend four hours or more a day watching television, and only twenty-seven percent of high school students engage in moderate physical activity at least thirty minutes a day on five or more days of the week.

- Three-quarters of overweight and obese nine- to thirteen-year-olds do not change their habits and remain overweight and obese in adulthood.

- Type 2 diabetes is on the rise in young people, a trend unheard of a decade ago.

Centers for Disease Control and Prevention, as reported in *USA Today;* July 17, 2002

caregivers at an early age. Others are angry at the parent, and perhaps shamed by the anger, yet they do not have the resources to deal with those feelings.

Consider the viewpoint of siblings of a child who is ill. Often, the needs of the healthy child are overlooked because of the large amounts of time spent with the child who is sick. Sometimes children feel responsible for the illness of another. "Did I cause this?" is often a concern of children (and also of parents).

Congregations can offer support by

- providing respite care for the healthy family members. When one of the members of our congregation was ill, we formed a volunteer group of friends who weekly came to the home and helped feed the one who was sick so that the rest of the family could eat a meal together and relax.

- providing information and transportation for children and youth. When a family is caught up in caring for someone who is ill, they may be unable to keep up with ongoing programs for children and youth. Phoning with information of upcoming events and providing transportation can allow young people to stay active in church ministries.

- locating support groups for families. Sometimes groups may be in the congregation, sometimes in the larger community. Helping families meet other families with similar life-changing events helps them feel less lonely and can increase their skills and knowledge.

- identifying ways the chronically ill family member can participate in community and church activities. Addressing needs of accessibility is a must.

- addressing faith needs and issues. For many families, faith is what shapes a family's perception of a chronic illness or death. Faith can be a source of strength, but illness can sometimes create a faith crisis. These families often need ministerial staff to be available to reflect with the family, to listen to their concerns, and to offer prayers and support.

Death of a Family Member

Watch just about any television program today or go to a movie and you will experience death. Yet, as a culture, we are still reluctant to face the inevitability of death and talk together about feelings and experiences when death occurs. Parents need to be aware of things that can happen as their child or youth tries to deal with the death of someone who is close to him or her. Parents may need to deal with

- sleep problems, both inability to sleep and seeking sleep when the child would have otherwise been engaged in activities;
- feelings of anger and aggression toward surviving family members and toward the family member who has died;
- refusal to follow normal routines;
- regression to past behaviors, such sucking thumbs (even for teens) or a slowing down of maturation;
- loss of self-confidence (particularly when an adult dies who has contributed to the child's self-confidence and self-esteem).

Millennial Voices

"After the suicide attempt, I realized how precious life is and how much it would hurt the people around me if I were gone from their lives."

Millennial Generation Survey, 2002

Pointers for Parents

- Believe that your child is capable of and could commit suicide.

- Watch for growing depression, dropping out of activities, pulling away from friends and family.

- Watch for behaviors such as giving away treasured items to friends and family.

- Do not be afraid to intervene.

People seem to have a perception that when someone dies, we plunge into a deep pit of grief and despair that lessens with each day until we are able to climb out of the pit. That is not true. Remember, we all have a different timetable in dealing with grief. Grieving is an up-and-down, day-by-day experience that takes time.

When children experience the death of a family member, their feelings of grief are often mixed with fear: *What will happen to me?* For youth, who see themselves and those they care about as immortal, death can create a crisis of belief.

Congregations can help by
• paying attention to each family member;
• talking about the loved one who has died;
• providing suggestions to families for remembering loved ones: creating memory books, writing poems, drawing pictures;
• offering classes and support groups for those who are grieving;
• providing books and brochures that help parents talk with their children and youth about death.

Divorce

Virtually all children assume some level of blame for a divorce. In addition to feelings of guilt, children also experience the same stages of grief adults do: shock, denial, bargaining, sadness, depression, anger, powerlessness, a sense of rejection, abandonment, isolation, and finally acceptance and hope. There does not seem to be any age at which it is easier for a child to handle divorce.

A congregation can help by
• offering divorce recovery programs for children, youth, and adults;
• buying and displaying appropriate books in the church library;
• pairing families newly experiencing divorce with families who have been through divorce;
• researching and offering to families information on community divorce support groups and counseling services;
• helping the divorcing partners in parenting beyond the divorce. (Children and youth are torn by feelings of loyalty when parents divorce. The attitudes of the adults are important in fostering health in their children. Children succeed when they feel free to stay in contact with and to love both parents.)

Substance Abuse

We live in a culture that says, "Feel bad? You don't have to! Just drink this drink, take this pill, or inject this drug into your veins." And from all evidence of youth culture, substances are easily available in schools, in communities, and in homes. Indeed, some families encourage drinking and other experimentation at home, reasoning that it is better for a child to experience these things in the home environment than to go out into the community seeking drugs or alcohol.

As congregations, we can train those who work with youth and parents to watch for behavior that might indicate drug or alcohol use. Some of the signs include
• presence of drug paraphernalia, including pipes, clips, razor blades, scales, mirrors, rolling papers;

- a marked difference in eating habits;
- a fall in school performance (even as slight as moving from an *A* to a *B* when a child has consistently made *A*'s all through school);
- changes in sleep patterns;
- vomiting;
- increased income or purchases beyond the child's known income;
- increase in violent behavior;
- dropping old friends;
- frequent use of eye drops.

Congregations who look seriously at this issue can
- provide up-to-date information on drug and alcohol use by children and youth;
- support parents and youth workers in actively seeking information about drugs and drug use;
- develop a plan of intervention for children and youth when drug or alcohol abuse is noted;
- include programs on drug and alcohol abuse in children's programming, instead of waiting until the teen years;
- provide listings of support groups, such as Al-Anon, and include information on when and where such groups meet.

Violence and Bullying

Recently, I watched a movie with my eleven-year-old son. Our first hurdle was finding a movie that was not rated R. When we did find a movie, the blurb led me to believe that we would be watching a feel-good movie about a young man coaching a baseball team. What I was unprepared for was the death of one of the young ball players, who was killed in a drive-by shooting. My child cried. I cried. The good thing, though, was that we talked about it—about the living conditions of children in our country, about his safety, and about our response to violence.

We live in an extremely violent world. We can see on any news program examples of people abusing and harming one another every day. In addition, television programs, electronic games, music, and movies also trade in the currency of violence. Because violence surrounds us, it has become an expectation of the environment rather than an exception. Children and youth today are participants in the violence, as bullying is an everyday occurrence in our schools.

Many children and youth experience violence in the home. Child abuse has not significantly dropped. And many children and youth witness violence in the home against their mothers. Children and youth who are abused struggle with feelings of guilt, self-blame, and low self-esteem. Many also become perpetrators of aggression against other family members or peers. These youth feel vulnerable, hopeless, and paralyzed by the violence.

What can we do? The starting point for every congregation is ensuring that the congregation is a safe place for children and youth. *Safe Sanctuaries: Reducing the Risk of Child Abuse in the Church* aids congregations in planning policies and procedures to prevent child abuse. *Safe Sanctuaries* includes suggested training and worship that addresses the ills of abuse.

DemoFacts

"The most impact is sexual abuse because now I see things in a different point of view than I did before. And now it is hard to trust any guy because it is hard to face it."

Millennial Generation Survey, 2002

What Your Church Can Do

The minimum expected protection requirement of churches and agencies when a charge of abuse occurs will be a background check performed before the person starts working with the children. If not, you will be held liable.

For parents, it is important in confronting violence to

- view television, movies, and video games with your child. Talk together about incidents and about other ways to resolve conflicts.
- reassure your children about ways you are helping keep them safe in the home and in the community.
- talk with teachers, principals, and other parents about situations in the schools. Even if you cannot volunteer in the school, you can advocate through parents who are on school boards.
- recognize that your child is touched by violence. Most children know of others who have experienced violence at home or at school. Do not ignore the issue; address it.

Sexuality

Recently, I was teaching a workshop for preschool teachers. I listened as they talked about ways three- and four-year-olds dress. Even at this young age, children are following the trends of teen stars and dressing in trendy, tight, sexy clothing. Through the media, children are exposed at a young age to images of sexuality and values related to sexuality. If the church is silent about sexuality and if parents are fearful of talking about sexuality because of questions they may be asked, children have no other recourse but to form opinions and values based on media images. Is that what we really believe as humans created in the image of God? If sexuality is an ignored issue, how can we help children and youth make faith-based decisions related to their bodies? If sexuality is a hidden issue in the family and at church, how do children and youth receive accurate information about sexuality?

Indeed, sexual experimentation begins at a young age. Without other information than what is shared in peer groups, our children and youth are left to make decisions that can harm them physically and psychologically. As a congregation, we can

- sponsor sexuality education classes at church using material such as *Before They Ask: Talking With Your Child About Sex From a Christian Perspective* (for parent groups), *Created by God: About Sexuality for Older Girls and Boys* (for fifth and sixth graders), and *Let's Be Real: Honest Discussions About Faith and Sexuality* (for youth).
- include decision-making discussions often in Sunday school and in youth groups. Encourage an atmosphere where children and youth can voice their struggles and receive encouragement for sound decisions.
- look at the media images of sexuality in magazines, books, articles, songs, movies, and music. Compare these to a faith stance of the sacredness of human life and respect for self and others.
- provide the resources of the church to those dealing with the consequences of decisions that have led to early pregnancy or sexually transmitted diseases. Many youth, in dealing with decisions that have led to pregnancy or disease, need the support of a caring group. Provide information about community resources and support for the youth as part of a loving congregation.
- address issues of sexual abuse and date rape. This past year a boy from my son's school was accused of raping a girl in the community. As a parent, it was hard for me to approach my fourteen-year-old and ask,

"What have you heard?" "What do you think?" "What is the kind, just, and loving approach in this situation?" Parents need help in feeling they can talk with their youth about these situations. Youth teachers and counselors need support in discussing such issues at church.

Disabilities

To be correct, the title of this section should be "People Who Have Disabilities." In every area of concern for people, the focus should be first on the person and then on the condition. This language reminds us of the ways we are all similar, even as it focuses on the ways that we are all different.

The struggle for families when one of its members has a disability is inclusion. Those with disabilities—no matter what the nature of the disability—often feel different, left out, not wanted, and not included. Families are often challenged as they try to meet the common human need of each family member to belong and to be part of a community.

To remind ourselves of what we are talking about in the area of disabilities, think of some of these disabling conditions. (Note: This list is not comprehensive, but it is illustrative.)

- learning disabilities
- attention deficit disorder (ADD)
- autism
- dyslexia
- Tourette's syndrome
- Down syndrome
- spina bifida
- cerebral palsy
- muscular dystrophy

Fewer than fifteen percent of disabilities are present at birth. The other eighty-five percent are acquired at some later point in the life cycle. Often, when people come into contact with those who have a disability, they react with pity or fear. They may ignore the person, discounting his or her presence and contribution. They may feel disgusted, feel impatient, or think, *We don't have time for this here.* This reaction can be particularly true in the church when dealing with learning disabilities or attention deficit disorder in small-group settings such as Sunday school.

A growing number of children and youth are receiving some form of medicinal therapy to control a condition, such as attention deficit disorder or Tourette's syndrome. Many of these drugs require a "vacation," so parents may not give the medication to their children on the weekend. Their behavior, controlled by the medication during the week, may not be controlled on weekends, when they are participating in church activities.

What is a congregation to do? Responding appropriately to those with disabilities and to their families struggling with their disabilities is especially important in our congregations. After all, our faith is based on community, and we talk about and try to act out of a mindset of forming and being formed in Christian community. Help your congregation take note of these suggestions:

Pointers for Parents

When difficult behaviors occur, are you led to look immediately at medicating your child instead of checking out other options to work with your child?

- Remember the person first. Remind yourself and others that all are children of God. We are all more than any type of disability we may have.
- Do not be afraid to ask real questions about disabilities, preferred interactions, and ways to accommodate children and youth for full participation in congregational life. The disability is real and has to be addressed. To ignore it shows disregard for the person.
- Educate all who work with, or are in a class or small group with, a person with a disability to ensure understanding and inclusion.
- Support parents. Discover community resources for parent support groups related to particular conditions.
- Work to help each child and youth find ways to be in ministry in the congregation. Remember the importance of acolyting, reading Scripture, drawing a bulletin cover, or being involved in mission trips. These same discipleship needs are shared by all, including those with a disability.

And the List Goes On

We could continue listing issues that tear at the family. As individuals and congregations who care for children, youth, and their families, we are called on not to ignore the hurt but to address the hurt. We are called to offer guidance where appropriate, to pray for one another, to engage in Christian conversation with one another, and to help one another find the resources needed to move through hurting situations.

What will you do?

Responding to the Needs of Parents

MaryJane Pierce Norton

You have probably pondered this before, but I invite you to think about it again: When we receive a new appliance, we also receive an instruction book that gives us operating instructions for the item, cautions, and a safety net in the form of a number to call if the item malfunctions. Each time I had a baby, I looked for the instruction manual. I could not locate one! And yet, the task of parenting is far more complicated than operating any appliance.

From the anticipation of the birth of the child through the child's adulthood, parents are called on to parent in a way that acknowledges the needs of the child. However, with each age of childhood, there are corresponding needs of parents. Those of us interested in ministries with the Millennial Generation must pay attention to the needs of the parents of these children and young people.

Unfortunately, the way we have organized for ministry has often been based on a schooling model. The careful attention paid to each age of children and young people may be a plus of this model. However, a corresponding weakness may be treating each age in isolation without acknowledging the connections in family. This includes not paying attention to the needs of parents at the corresponding ages of children. Note that these parenting needs are not based on the ages of the parents. Indeed, these parenting needs are equally applicable to a grandparent, aunt, uncle, or foster parent raising a child.

The stages of parenthood correspond with the ages of their children. Thus, a parent with multiple children will be in more than one stage at the same time. Parents must recognize this reality and adapt their parenting styles to match the stage of each child.

Phases of parenthood are generalizations. Parents may experience all, some, or none of the characteristics. The phases are outlined here to help the parent assess his or her own needs as related to the children and realize what the needs of each child will be.

First Phase: "I will be the perfect parent!"

After I discovered I was pregnant, but before I actually gave birth, I had great visions of the parent I would be. I also had great visions for my yet-to-be-born child. Of course, he or she would be smart, good looking, respectful, and talented. I would be calm, fun to be around, always ready to share my faith and help my child grow. My child would fall asleep when put to bed and wake up pleasant and ready for each day. What a fantasy!

While preparing to receive a child, whether by birth or by adoption, such thoughts are common. It is a time for imagining. It is also common in this stage for prospective parents to be fearful: to think they know nothing, to think they are unprepared, and to think they cannot possibly raise a child.

This stage of preparation often reflects the parenting styles experienced by a prospective parent. One who has yet to give birth hears how a friend allows her children to crawl into bed with them night after night and says, "I will never allow my children to sleep in our bed." Another remembers his own father and says, "I won't miss the baseball games of my daughter because of work." Or, "I won't be the kind of parent who talks about my child all the time."

While usually reflecting on what we *will not* do, these imaginings also include what we will do based on positive parenting we have seen or experienced. Prospective parents may vow to play with their child as their mother had played with them. They may vow to take their child to church as they were taken when young. More of these statements may be made in anticipation of the first child. However, even with a second, third, fourth, prospective parents will make statements about what they will or will not do with this child that they failed to do or enjoy doing with other children in the home.

These tasks are to be accomplished during this imagining phase:

- Say to your partner what you think is important as a parent. For single parents, it is helpful to have another adult with whom to reflect on values and to ask for feedback.
- Prepare for the birth/receiving a baby: gather what is needed for the child, prepare a place in the home for the child, reflect on your own attitude as a parent.
- Name some of the important markers anticipated for the birth of the child: decisions about baptism, childcare, involvement of extended family, and celebrations such as Thanksgiving and Christmas.

Second Phase: "It wasn't supposed to be like this!"

This stage relates to the infant, toddler, and preschool years of children. Immediately after the birth or adoption of an infant and the euphoria of the first days, parents move into a sleep-deprived state driven by the constant needs of the infant. New parents can be overwhelmed with all the tasks of caring for an infant. They are astounded at the number of diapers used, the number of feedings needed, the time required for holding, rocking, and caressing the infant. Exhaustion is always just one step away for parents when their children are in these early years. This exhaustion can and does lead to depression for some parents. It is important for congregations to be aware of this possibility and plan to be supportive of parents.

As the child grows, parents often become absorbed in the growth of the child. Many parents eagerly talk about visits to the pediatrician, where they are reassured about the child's growth and carefully plot each stage of development.

Even when it is a second or third child, parents at this phase of parenthood have a feeling of freshness and newness. Watching the unfolding growth of the child and seeing the world with the new eyes of a young child can be a source of wonder and joy for a parent.

And yet, holding onto an identity separate from that of parent can be difficult. Life can become an endless routine of caregiving tasks, and parents may lose sight of their own needs. The tasks of bonding with and caring for the child while caring for self and a partner are time consuming and often produce tension. Parenting aids—books, videos, and small-group studies—can be helpful.

Childcare is often an issue, so finding the options for childcare in a community is another area where parents seek help. As the child grows and develops his or her own opinions, issues arise around authority and discipline. Again, parents may look to the congregation for help with these needs.

Even with the needs of care that are heavy at this age, parents often think they can learn to handle their child easily enough. They are not yet worried about the bigger issues of alcohol and drug abuse, sexual experimentation, and skipping school.

Third Phase: "I'm just the taxi driver."

This phase of parenthood relates to the childhood through preteen years. The activity level of children grows rapidly in these years. They are independent, so they can dress themselves, feed themselves, and so forth; however, they are active and involved in a variety of activities. Parents find themselves entering fully into the phase of transporting their children to music, sports, church, and so forth.

Related to this new role as taxi driver, parents face decisions on how to interpret for their children what is going on in the wider world. They have responsibilities for setting limits on such things as television, Internet, and video games. What started as a harmless activity of putting a video in for the three-year-old child and letting him or her watch alone while the parent performed household tasks now becomes an activity of self-choice. The parent must take time to be aware of what her or his children are watching or playing.

Conversations that help the child interpret the world (what is right, what is wrong, and why) are important for children, but these conversations can be scary for parents. The church can help by forming a small group of parents who are struggling with these same issues.

Another emerging issue with children this age is their encounter with gender identification and sexuality. Even though we may talk freely with our child about political beliefs or current affairs, parents find it difficult to discuss sexuality. Parents may not feel that they are alone if the church has a lending library with resources to suggest and parenting groups where they can talk about these topics.

Equally scary can be talking with a child about faith issues. We know, however, that these kinds of conversations are important for faith formation of the child. Helping parents establish devotional times in the home, pray with their children, and talk about faith is an important task for the congregation.

Parents of school-age children also need to help children with the task of learning. School is where children receive their identity, see themselves as productive or not, and see themselves as smart or not.

What Your Church Can Do

When looking at faith in the home, congregations can help by providing printed resources, videos and books in a lending library, specially prepared services, sermon illustrations and newsletter articles on the following:
- practicing home devotions;
- praying together as a family;
- providing rituals for celebrating Advent, Christmas, Lent, Easter, and Pentecost;
- having ongoing conversations on faith issues.

Fourth Phase: "My child is embarrassed by me."

This phase corresponds with preadolescence into late teens. Parents of children this age feel that they have lost control. The growing independence of teens means they are going places parents do not always know about with people parents do not know. Parents say, "When I asked her how school was today, she said, 'Fine.'" "When I asked him what he did, he replied 'Stuff.'" These answers make the parent think he or she does not know what is going on the child's life. As the child grows, both the child and the parent fear change.

The following are important tasks related to parenting teens:

- Stay connected with the child. Teens, while giving parents little feedback, still want to be part of the family and be connected into the life of the family. They make it difficult for parents, but parents of teens can find help in small support groups.
- Remember, the parent still has authority. Many children will say, when asking permission, "You really don't want me to do this, do you?" In this way, they are hinting to a parent that they want the parent to set boundaries for their safety.
- Continue to state the values of the family and to engage the child in conversation. Attending church regularly, talking about faith in the home, praying together, and sharing in traditions help the teen stay connected.
- Realize that you and your child are separate. Since parents remember their teen years much more vividly than their preschool years, they are likely to project onto their child their own thoughts and feelings. A struggle for parents is to realize that what they did as a teen may or may not be what their teen will do.

Fifth Phase: "My baby has left home."

When a child reaches late teens into the twenties, many leave the household and establish one of their own. Many parents struggle with the empty-nest syndrome, especially if this is the last child to leave. Adults who have defined themselves totally as parents feel a sense of loss, a devaluing of who they are as individuals, and sometimes depression. Others rejoice at rediscovered freedom and enjoy this phase of exploring their own wants and needs. It can also be a time of rejoicing on the part of parents because their young-adult children now see the parents as smart again.

But balanced against this is the struggle to let go. Parents of young adults do not know what their children are doing, where they are, or how they occupy their time. It is a time of both fear and release.

Tasks in parenting young adults include these:

- redefining the parent/child relationship into adult to adult;
- rediscovering partner/partner relationships;
- reconciling yourself to the fact that your young-adult child will make his or her own choices;
- continuing emotional support;
- sometimes continuing economic support.

What Your Church Can Do

In all of these phases of parenthood, the congregation can be supportive by

- providing parenting literature for every stage of the development of children and youth;
- providing small support groups where parents can talk about issues related to raising children and youth;
- publishing information on community support for parents;
- recognizing that parents of children at different ages will be struggling between parenting styles needed to fit each age of their children;
- supporting the faith formation of parents and helping them support their child's faith formation.

Out-Familying Pseudo-Family Organizations

Terry B. Carty

Cults, Gangs, Street Organizations, and Paramilitary Units

Jerome had never shown signs of violence. His grades had been good, but his teachers reported that he was quiet and seemed to have few friends. His grandmother had made a good home for him after his mom had died and his father had left the state to find work. One of Jerome's junior high teachers began to notice that he had an unusual number of small injuries. When the teacher called Jerome's grandmother, his grandmother said that Jerome was rarely at home anymore. He had quit talking to her almost altogether. Today, Jerome is fifteen years old and is being tried as an adult for murdering an elderly woman, an initiation requirement for his street organization.

Cheron has not been seen or heard from for two years. Originally, her parents were encouraged when she found new religious friends. As a family, they were not involved in religion, although both parents had gone to church in their childhood. Cheron's parents hoped that these new friends would help Cheron develop some of the respectful values they had learned in church. By the time they realized that she was becoming more distant from them, it was too late. They argued with Cheron; then Cheron left. The police suspect that the cult changed her name and appearance and transported her to a location far from home.

Cults, gangs, street organizations, and paramilitary units are now in every size and type of community. Once established, these organizations are almost impossible to defeat. Community leaders cannot defeat them simply by making laws and trying to enforce them. Church leaders cannot defeat them simply by preaching and praying about it. Families cannot keep their children safe simply by putting restrictions on them. These organizations cannot be defeated by physical strength, by conventional reasoning, or by civilized methods. People are always hurt by these organizations and by forcible efforts to eradicate them.

The only way to eliminate these groups is to eliminate their supply of new members. Families, congregations, and communities can defeat these organizations by out-familying them.

The Pseudo-Family Organization (PFO)

All human beings come into this world with basic needs: physical, psychological, and social. In Creation, God planned for these needs to be met. God designed human reproduction to involve two humans, a male and a female, to start human life. At least one of them (the

---

Signs of Street Organization or Gang Activity

- Graffiti
- Tattoos
- Branding
- Cigarette burns
- Scars
- Bruises
- Unexplained income
- Increased time away from home

mom) is naturally present when a child takes the first breath. God also created humans with a natural tendency to live in society with other people, with the family at the core.

In this article, we will call an organization that replaces the family with an imitation a *pseudo-family organization (PFO)*. These organizations existed in ancient Sparta, where children were removed from their families to become part of a military family. Orphanages and company towns have attempted to substitute for the familial needs of people. These organizations met necessary human needs in order to accomplish their primary goals of building an army, caring for displaced children, or manufacturing a product. Generally, though, their primary goal was not the fulfillment of human need.

Today, dangerous PFOs use human need to attract and hold young people in their control. Gangs, street organizations, paramilitary units, and religious cults have found that by satisfying basic humans needs, they can attract people who have not found their place in normal society or who are missing some important family elements in their lives. However, these PFOs are interested in controlling and using their members, not in their human fulfillment. PFOs attract people because they offer what new members desperately need: safety and belonging. After someone is recruited into the organization, he or she is guided to loyalty and dependence, rather than toward independence and fulfillment.

In the late 1960's Abram Maslow published his theories of human development that were based on his sociological studies of people who were well adjusted in life (*self-actualized* is his term). Some of the characteristics of someone he considered to be self-actualized were tolerance of others, lack of shame or anxiety about self, in touch with reality, experiencing joy, sense of discovery, creativity, sense of humor (but not making fun of others), need for privacy, and deep, personal relationships. He revealed five levels of development related to the fulfillment of human need. Note, though, that a functioning family does not need to know about Maslow's theories to fulfill the needs of its members. Likewise, most PFOs have not studied Maslow, but they have figured out that they can attract members by providing what a poorly functioning or absent family does not. As we look at Maslow's levels of development, it is easy to understand how a healthy, fully functioning family would satisfy these needs.

Maslow's Five Levels of Development Related to Needs
- Physical
- Safety
- Love and Belonging
- Respect
- Self-Actualization

Level One: Physical Needs

Survival is the most basic of needs. It includes the physical needs for food, water, oxygen, sleep, elimination of waste, and sex. Maslow thought that someone must have these physical survival needs substantially met (about eighty percent) before he or she could be ready for the next level of development.

Throughout history, cultures have discovered that they could keep people in slavery by controlling their basic needs. The initiation rituals of many PFOs include the withholding of food, water, sleep, and other basic needs. Some groups even include elements of asphyxiation to impress upon the initiate his or her powerlessness in the essential function of breathing. Through control of these needs, the powerful people make the subject physically dependent on them for survival.

Level Two: Safety Needs

In order to feel free from anxiety and chaos, a person needs a stable and predictable environment. He or she must feel relatively safe from immediate or future threat of harm. A person in the midst of battle or hanging from a ledge thinks of nothing else but finding a safe place. Maslow theorized that this level of need must be substantially met before one could progress to another level of fulfillment.

In many communities young people live under the threat of deadly violence. The crackle of gunfire is followed by bullets crashing through the walls of the homes of the innocent. Murder looms as the third leading cause of death for elementary- and junior-high-school-aged children. In every community, television and movies have brought the threat of violence to life-size proportions for children and youth. Even in the safest of communities, young people arm themselves with guns, knives, martial arts weapons, pieces of baseball bats, and other more crudely fashioned weapons. Most teens today do not think that their families or their homes can protect them from the danger they perceive around them.

Successful PFOs offer their members protection from the dangers they fear the most. Gangs and paramilitary groups offer the strength of numbers and weaponry. They take care of their members and retaliate when one of theirs is threatened, protect their territories, and demand loyalty from their membership. Cults often create the illusion that their members are safe because they are insulated from outside society and are no longer a part of the dangerous, chaotic world. Protection is a major offering of any PFO.

Level Three: Love and Belonging Needs

After one feels secure about survival and safety, the need for belonging and love emerges. This level of human need includes the feeling of acceptance, the feeling of being loved by others, and the need to be with others rather than be alone. If this critical need is denied in childhood and adolescence, it is likely to never be fulfilled in adulthood.

Generally, family culture in the United States creates an environment that is less likely to fulfill the needs for love and belonging than in the past. Parents' vocations remove them from the home for lengthy periods of time. Divorce rates have risen, and the number of single-parent families has increased. It is less likely that grandparents, aunts, uncles, and other extended family are in close contact with children. Schools, where students spend more time than with a parent, are being insulated from the rest of a child's society.

When people are surprised that a young person has been attracted to an PFO, the attraction is usually because of the unmet need for love and belonging. Physical and safety needs may have been well maintained, but the practices of a healthy family that nurture love and belonging may have been absent. These young people respond to the feeling of love that they get from being part of the brotherhood or sisterhood of the organization. Unfortunately, the drug culture is often mistaken for friendships; sex is often mistaken for love.

Level Four: Respect Needs

Closely related to love and belonging is self-esteem. Some people never reach the point in development at which they feel respected. Some never fully respect themselves. One developmental function in adolescence is the formation of self-image. Self-image is often unpredictable, affected by many factors that are unknown to parents or even to the teen. The way teens view themselves may be far different from the image that is visible to others.

When someone fails to develop a positive feeling about self, he or she may seek to improve his or her self-image in alternative ways. Some young people pride themselves on practicing body mutilation, such as excessive tattoos, piercings, and intentional scarring. Some pride themselves on being underachievers. These young people are prime targets for street organizations and cults that offer them a substitute for self-worth in reward systems. The powerful reward them for obedience with money, status, cars, stereos, other material goods, or even sexual favors. These tokens are often mistaken for respect.

Level Five: Self-Actualization Needs

The need to be a healthy, creative, contributing member of society is frequently never approached by a young person who becomes involved in an PFO. If the PFO's members were to reach this level of need, those types of organizations could not function. Self-actualizing people are not fulfilled receiving tokens instead of respect, sex and drugs instead of love and friendship, or fear instead of security.

PFOs carefully guard against self-actualization by creating the illusion that the outside world hates them and is not to be trusted. As a result, members of PFOs usually have poor communication skills, are territorial, control by violence, and undergo initiation rituals to prove loyalty. The leaders of these organizations demand that loyalty be unconditional. They try to assure the welfare and safety of the members by having a well-ordered business plan, with a chain of command that is broken only at extreme danger. They recruit primarily from low-income groups, outcasts, and loners. Their recruits are not likely to ever understand the concept of self-actualization.

Strategies That Work

Strategies that work are ones that starve PFOs of new members. When families function to meet the developmental needs of young people, there is no need for PFOs. It is important for communities and individuals to develop strategies to strengthen families and to supplement where families are incomplete. These strategies should center on meeting the needs of young people in healthy ways.

Strengthen Families

Communities can focus on families and values that are consistent with meeting developmental needs of young people. Law enforcement, schools, churches, entertainment, and businesses should see themselves as supplemental to established family structures in meeting these needs. They should empower, support, and encourage the efforts of parents to develop stronger families.

Strategies to strengthen families may include parenting classes; public service announcements that teach parents, schools, and churches teaching skills that help young people communicate their needs to parents; or community programs and churches teaching (or reminding) families of their purpose in the lives of young people.

Families need to be supported, and family members need to learn to support one another. They need to be empowered by society and to learn to empower one another within the family. They need to learn and teach healthy understandings of boundaries and expectations for each member. They should be taught constructive use of time. Many families need to be taught and supported in peaceful problem-solving skills in order to overcome generations of poor parenting practice. Some areas that need improvement in many families are

- modeling by parents and extended family members the life they expect of their children;
- focusing less on making money and more on providing a safe, secure home for the family; that is, do not let money be the goal;
- helping children discover gifts and interests and, as they mature, helping them develop their gifts and interests as potential careers in which they can find honorable, legal ways to earn a comfortable living;
- being helpful to children's efforts to become respected adults. (Efforts to make children and youth pull themselves up by the bootstraps or to toughen them up often drive young people into the arms of PFOs, where they can feel successful.)

Supplement Broken or Incomplete Families

Families today come in many configurations. Numerous models have replaced the nuclear family, once the primary model for family structure. Our challenge is to make all the models work to meet the needs of their members.

Supplementing the family with surrogate family members can often help. Surrogates are people from outside the family who become like family as they help young people find fulfillment. One family may need a father figure, while another may need grandparents. If family, friends, congregations, and communities are fully aware of one another, they will find that they complete one another. A relationship between an elderly person and a young family that has moved far away from home can provide the nurturing that both need. A parent can enter partnerships with teachers, coaches, or clergy that will bring more of a complete family environment into the lives of the children.

It is popular to recommend that people mentor young people. However, few people are adequately prepared to be mentors, and few organizations are effective in matching young people with adult mentors. Community and church organizations can be effective by developing strategies for creating the links between young people and adult mentors and by establishing training programs that are easily accessible for adults who are willing to be in an ongoing relationship with a young person.

Even people who are hesitant to become mentors can be effective role models. One can never fully know when a young person is looking

Model Peaceful Conflict Resolution

- Be assertive and fair.

- Speak in a calm and respectful tone of voice.

- Do not physically touch someone who is angry (unless restraint is necessary).

- Leave space for someone to walk away from an argument.

- Seek solutions that leave no losers; that is, everyone wins.

to him or her as a potential model for life. Most adults need some training in order to be intentional about modeling the kind of values that are not modeled by leaders of PFOs. They should model a commitment to learning, a value for the lives and welfare of other people, competency in social skills, effective peaceful conflict resolution, and an overall positive identity within the community.

An attitude for advocacy begins with unconditional acceptance. Generally, people with the most trouble have the most need. Our unconditional acceptance is proof of God's love for them.

But advocacy is more than acceptance; advocacy must have content. We must insist that society meet the physical, psychological, and social needs of young people. A young person may experience love and acceptance but still turn to an PFO because he or she has no hope of ever being able to earn an honest living. Communities and congregations must strive to create a web of support for young people that can make them feel protected and supported while preparing them for a reasonable expectation for an honorable and fulfilling future life. This type of support system could blunt the need for protection by PFOs.

Such a web does not need a master plan in order to begin to succeed. It needs only people who want to reach out to young people. Individuals and groups can be parts of such a web when they

- offer alternative programs, such as recreation, education, or creative activities;
- develop ministries that help people get personally involved with individual young people: sports, missions, music, classes for self-improvement (life skills), and small businesses;
- build one-on-one relationships or become mentors and ask, "What do I do well? What young person do I know who might like to learn this from me?";
- make a point of seeking and engaging young people in their own environment: workplace, fast-food restaurants, street corners, parking lots, basketball courts, or home;
- develop opportunities for young people to serve in meaningful ways: home repair, community fix-up (such as playground maintenance), painting buildings (try a mural), youth mentoring older people in things new to culture (computers, programming VCRs, telephone features);
- develop employment: create jobs for young people that both train and pay them a reasonable wage; encourage friends to create jobs, hire gang members, promote young people to positions of responsibility and importance.

The Church as Family

Robert D. Pierson

Science fiction has become real life, and everything seems possible for the Millennial Generation. This generation is growing up in a time with great possibilities but also great challenges. The advance in technology of this electronic, biochemical age is sometimes beyond our imagination. The Millennial Generation is growing up in a time of peril and uncertainty: Children are shooting children, and wars are being waged that are beyond definition and beyond solution. The threat of nuclear, biological, or chemical terrorism is constant.

The Millennial Generation is growing up in families that are as varied as the culture in which they live. Their family context today is so varied that it is impossible to provide categories to describe them. The family models in which the Millennials live include single parents with live-in mates; never-married moms with adopted children; grandparents raising grandchildren; blended families with yours, mine, ours, and somebody else's; divorced children returning to their parents' homes with several kids and lots of chaos; several under-employed adults living together with their kids; and old-style nuclear families. In this changed environment of the family, the Millennial Generation seeks to find meaning, direction, and community.

By responding to the needs of children and youth, the church creates the opportunity not only to strengthen the family unit, whatever configuration it may be, but also to serve as the extended family of these children and youth and their parents. As these young people grow to become adults, the church can provide the model for community relationships built on Christ's concepts of love.

The Changing Nature of Family

To understand the church's role in the midst of this new environment, we need first to understand the changing nature of family. For most of human history, families were like clans. Abraham and Isaac moved their clans of several generations back and forth across the Promised Land. People needed to live together with multigenerational and many-faceted families to provide the labor force and economic power for survival.

As the Industrial Age of the late 1800's developed, we could function as extended families. Parents, grandparents, aunts, uncles, and cousins moved westward together in the pioneer spirit. They farmed in cooperation and developed family businesses that could be financed and operated with the sharing of resources. Children were part of a big family that essentially had many parents.

With the end of the Depression and the beginning of the Second World War, the nuclear family became the model. Mom, Dad, and two kids could live in a "Leave It to Beaver" home with success. The division of labor was clear, and the children had a sense of stability.

Yet, the diversified economy of the Second World War was the demise of the nuclear family. During the Second World War, the need for women to be employed outside the home for the war effort began the movement from the nuclear family as the basic economic unit to the one-person economic unit. The movement for human rights provided for independence, and divorce was financially more possible.

With the sexual revolution of the 1960's, monogamous relationships became less and less the standard of our society. Though the church stood against extramarital and premarital sex, these have become the cultural practice of the twenty-first century. The prosperity of the last half of the twentieth century and the explosion of choice and freedom have created an entitlement society. Baby Boomers and Postmoderns believe they are entitled to multiple choices, continual growth, and the right to have it all. With this mindset, loyalty and family responsibility have become almost unpopular.

The contemporary American culture is excitement-addicted, prosperous, and highly stimulated. Many people are more interested in having a good time and getting ahead than they are in caring for kids, giving quality time to anyone within the family or within any relationship, and holding onto the values that were once a foundation of family life. Consequently, Baby Boomers, Postmoderns, and the Millennials find themselves highly stimulated and lonely beyond imagination.

The Church as the New Extended Family

At the time of the great missionary movement of the 1800's, the church saw itself as mobilizing to bring the gospel to the heathens around the world. In the time of the social gospel of the twentieth century, the church saw itself as the vehicle of social justice to a corrupt society and world. In the twenty-first century, the Millennial Generation needs the church to be family. It is time for the church to respond aggressively to this desperate cry.

In the varied environment of family life, the church today can provide practical models for relationships, values, and support. The church can be the new extended family in partnership with the multiplicity of family designs present in society. The church can teach models of respect, relationships, values, beliefs, and ideals that can provide for youth and children the content for their model for family in the future.

To meet this challenge of encouraging and developing models for the family, the church must understand the issues of family development. Research has isolated forty basic assets that children and youth need today. In the past, most of these assets were provided by the nuclear family, extended family, or the clan. These basic assets include such items as

DemoFacts

Other than your family or friends, which most influences the choices you make?

41%   Church/Temple/Mosque
37%   School
19%   Media (TV, radio, etc.)
 3%   Government

Millennial Generation Survey, 2002

- positive family communications
- older-adult relationships
- service to others
- boundaries
- adult role models
- positive peer influence
- high expectations
- creative activities
- motivation
- encouragement
- caring
- social justice
- honesty
- integrity
- responsibility
- restraint
- planning
- competence
- resilience
- conflict resolution
- personal power
- self-esteem
- a sense of purpose

The forty assets could be summarized under three categories:
1. the need for affirmation
2. the need for community
3. the need for purpose

The Need for Affirmation

Affirmation, community, and purpose are assets the church has sought to teach throughout its history. These are assets that can be conveyed in the extended family of the church and passed on in the redevelopment of the family by the Millennials.

Affirmation is described by psychologists and behavioral therapists in terms of self-esteem, self-worth, ego needs, and a sense of well-being. The way in which self-esteem and security are developed in the child or adult is by being loved. Self-esteem is often a function of unconditional love: knowing we are loved even when we make mistakes. When the family consists of so few members that it cannot continually provide support, children and adults go elsewhere for community, self-esteem, and support. When the family itself becomes dysfunctional, when there is anger and resentment, when people go through divorce, it is nearly impossible to communicate unconditional love and affirmation. This leads children to seek affirmation, security, and self-esteem from other sources. Everything from drug cultures to sporting events become means by which they try to find acceptance.

Affirmation is a product of quality church life. It is the church that can best supply the self-esteem through unconditional love. First Corinthians 13:4-8 tells us how to provide affirmation. To be loving as Christ taught is, first, to be patient. Too often, however, our approach to relationships is a quick fix, instant gratification. The church with its understanding of time, knowing that God's time is eternity, can help people tear away the instantaneous mindset of the present generations and learn real patience. Real affirmation does not happen in a romantic glance across a crowded room but takes time, long periods of caring, loving, supporting, and helping.

The second requirement of 1 Corinthians 13 is kindness. Affirmation happens when you care enough to be kind. The family and the church family can be the environment of both teaching and showing this kindness.

Paul also describes a whole set of behaviors that are not loving. Self-esteem is destroyed when we are envious, boastful, arrogant, rude, irritable, and resentful. These characteristics of contemporary relationships are like terrorist activities to human self-esteem. When we are resentful, arrogant, ill-mannered, unkind, conceited, and selfish, we emotionally kill the people around us. These negative behaviors must be fought against and corrected by the church as a family. To be the new family, the church must do what it believes in. Clergy, laity, teachers, leaders, and committed families must aggressively stand against the enemies of true affirmation and community. We must live up to the standards of treating one another with love.

The church as family needs to be a place where we are affirmed, where our goodness is celebrated. The church needs to be the place where we come and sense clearly that God loves us. Church should be where children and teens love to be, because there they feel good about themselves. Church should be one of the places where we keep the record of the good. Newsletters, church bulletins, Sunday school classes, worship services should be contacts of affirmation. The church is the family that can provide and teach affirmation. Living out of that understanding, the church will provide the basic necessary ingredients for helping children and adults have a sense of self-esteem.

The Need for Community

Community may become the most longed for and desperately needed aspect in the life of Baby Boomers, Postmoderns, and Millennials. With the fragmentation of the family and the instability of the basic institutions of our society, we long for community. For Baby Boomers, this was represented by the television sitcom *Cheers*, a place where "everybody knows your name." The long-running TV series *Friends* offers Postmoderns the picture of a community of friends who accept, care for, and love one another; interact and react; and are always there for one another. As with Postmoderns and Baby Boomers, Millennials need community and are doing everything in their power, in a fragmented world, to create it.

Community in the past has been found through family, friendships, and other close relationships. The demise of family and the rise of individualism has impacted Postmoderns and Millennials with a terrible, pervasive sense of loneliness. New communities have been created around sports, recreation, parties, sex, hobbies, business, and finance.

The church, by its nature, is community. From the first description of the church at the end of Acts 2 to the detailed description in 1 Corinthians 12, the church is a place of acceptance, caring, and community. Paul defines the church as "the body of Christ," diverse yet united, each part functioning differently and yet with a commonness of goal, purpose, and identity. Now is a critical time for the church to be what it was created to be: community or family for each generation. When Paul says in Romans 13 that all the laws of the prophets can be summarized as love, we understand that this must be community. Children come to church to be with people who care and understand. Children's Sunday school classes, youth groups, fellowship, choir, and mission teams are places where people should feel they are in family. The model Paul presents of the church is a church with diverse participants, yet each one knowing he or she is important. Children, youth, and adults of all ages need to know that in the church they are accepted and are part of the community. People with leadership skills, along with those whose lives seem to be totally dysfunctional, must come to know that together, in the church, we are family.

The Need for Purpose

Purpose has long been understood as a major need of a healthy person. We need to know that we are not a waste of time, that we have a reason for being. Too often, families cannot give members such a sense of direction or purpose. However, purpose is the defining aspect of the life of the church. Consequently, the church is in a powerful place to provide this sense of purpose to the members of its family.

Jesus called the disciples to come and follow him, telling them that their purpose would be to make disciples. In Luke 4, Jesus defines his own purpose. It is inherent to those who take up their cross and follow Jesus Christ that we have a mission, a purpose, and a reason for being. That reason for being is conveyed in the family of the church. Children can learn from the time they are young that they were born with a purpose, a reason for being. Love and justice are a part of the calling of every Christian. Christians are called, as the children of God, to do God's work.

A sense of purpose in life is a defining difference between people who are more resilient, are happier, have greater energy, have a better sense of humor, and are able to withstand all kinds of difficulty, and those who are not. A sense of purpose gives us strength and focus to endure and do what must be done.

In the pioneer times, people lived out their purpose in establishing a new frontier and new possibilities for a growing nation. Farm families during the Depression knew their purpose was survival. In the nuclear families of the 1950's, the purpose was to get the country going again, get ahead financially, and embrace the American dream of owning your own home and a car. Today, weakened family structures struggle to give participants in the family a sense of purpose. When the contemporary families, in all the varieties of models, link themselves into the church, they mobilize the energy and efforts of a whole group of families in becoming a new united family, an extended family of spiritual proportions. It is the gospel of Jesus Christ that gives today's family purpose, direction, values, and ideals.

The Church Must Be Family

In a society where terrorism, environmental collapse, and economic downturns create instability in all generations, the Millennial Generation sees half its families coming apart in divorce. It is imperative that these families be part of the community of faith. The church can be family where there is affirmation, support, community, and encouragement. The church can be family where our purpose is presented regularly in Christian education and worship. The church can be family

DemoFacts

In your church, how do you rate the following (5=highest, 1=lowest)?

Youth Program

5	4	3	2	1
46%	28%	14%	7%	5%

Service (to those in need)

5	4	3	2	1
43%	30%	18%	8%	1%

Preaching

5	4	3	2	1
32%	33%	25%	7%	3%

Worship

5	4	3	2	1
25%	34%	31%	7%	2%

Church School

5	4	3	2	1
22%	32%	28%	11%	7%

Teaching You to Pray

5	4	3	2	1
19%	29%	27%	18%	8%

Youth '99 Survey of United Methodist Youth, General Board of Discipleship

What Your Church Can Do

- Teach classes for parents and other interested adults using the resource *What Kids Need to Succeed: Proven, Practical Ways to Raise Good Kids,* by Peter L. Benson, Judy Galbraith, and Pamela Espeland.

- Pair youth with adults as prayer partners at various times of the year.

- Think of ways the congregation can identify key points of life change in children's lives and develop rites of passage. For example, giving a third-grade Bible or praying with youth when they receive their driver's license.

where there is a sense of identity and direction. We know today that so many of the assets that children need to grow up strong are assets that can be provided only by caring, loving people who are there to help, to encourage, and to discipline. The church can be those people.

Whether the churches are mega-churches, small county-seat town churches, or fragile churches in declining neighborhoods, they can become the families of tomorrow. It is inherent in the gospel of Jesus Christ that a message of hope, love, purpose and security is expressed. The problems of the church of the past must be overcome with new models that allow the church to be its best at a time that it is desperately needed to be family.

We must understand that for the church to be family, it is not only responding to the desperate need of the Millennial Generation but is also preserving its own future. The great evangelist of The Methodist Church, Harry Denman, often said that the church was only one generation away from extinction. That generation is today's Millennial Generation. If the church of the future will become family, it will give this generation what they so desperately need. For the church to become family for the Millennial Generation, the church will continue as truly God's own people, powerful and strong, for new generations, for new challenges, and for new opportunities.

Section Three

Millennials and Their World

HHS Secretary Tommy G. Thompson today released a new report showing that high school students are acting more responsibly by avoiding tobacco, marijuana, risky sexual behavior, and other potentially dangerous behaviors that increase their risk for injury, illness, and death.

"The youth in our high schools are increasingly acting like responsible young men and women—making responsible choices that will protect themselves now and well into the future," Secretary Thompson said. "At the same time, this report shows that too many teenagers continue to engage in risky behaviors. All of us—teachers, community leaders, celebrities, politicians, and especially parents—must work harder to prepare our children with the knowledge and confidence that they need to make wise decisions."

Centers for Disease Control and Prevention press release; June 27, 2002

Dear Diary

Kelly Welty

At the turn of the millennium, some high school students around the country were asked to keep an audio diary of their thoughts as New Year's Day 2000 dawned. They were asked to record their thoughts before and after the New Year. Remember, we had questions about Y2K and wondered what the future would bring. Kelly's diary illuminates a number of issues and concerns that members of her generation face on a daily basis.

December 22, 4:00 p.m.

Here in Spencer not a lot goes on. It's kinda quiet and calm, and it seems like everyone in my school, every kid growing up in this town, has this dream to be someone, to go somewhere, and to do something: see the world. But it seems like they never make it....

And the best thing they can tell us to do is to follow our dreams. That's what my parents and neighbors and everyone seems to tell me and everyone around me. Follow your dreams.

Well, following your dreams is great if you know what your dreams are. If you don't know exactly what you wanna be, what you wanna do, I think that's when you set yourself up for failure, because you can change your mind so easily, and it can mess up your life....

I was discussing this with some of my friends and classmates, and it's unbelievable to talk to them because they feel the exact same way, but no one has ever said it.

December 30, 6:00, in my room

My family

My brother's funny. I don't know how to describe him. He makes everyone laugh. He is very, very funny. And he doesn't listen to my parents a lot, which is okay with me because it makes life more exciting. My dad is a regional manager for a soda company. That's kinda cool because we always have soda and have parties and stuff, which is fun. My mom is a very social person. She has a lot of friends, knows a lot of people. She works for the post office. She is definitely very strict with us. She is used to having her complete way, which is okay, I guess, because we're used to it. I've lived in the same house, in the same town, my whole life. That is good because I know the people; I have the same friends. It makes us really tight. I'm glad of that.

December 30 (continued)

My biggest fears and hopes for the future

I think my future hope is just to be happy. What more can you ask for? I mean, you don't know what's going to happen, so if you just hope to be happy, then you will be, pretty much. And if you go into it with that positive attitude, you're always going to be happy. I mean, there's no other option, because that's what's going to happen. If you say, "I'm going to be happy," then whatever is thrown at you, you're going to be happy. It's great. I love that attitude, and I wish I could make more people have it. But, you know, I don't think they get it.

My fear for the future is losing control. I know now that it's my fault if I'm in control and screw up, and I can deal with the consequences. If someone screws up and messes up my life and everything, then that's crazy. And I can't recover because I need to know that if I work really hard and do my best, then I'm going to succeed—because it's part of the American dream. I'm in the honors class at my school, which is like the top members of the class. We're supposed to be the brightest kids at our school. I'm in the best class ever to go through this school…. It's pretty exciting to be part of a group like that. But I'll never forget the first day of my honors humanities class (history and English combined), when the teacher stood up in front of the room and asked, "What do you guys think the American dream is?" Now, you have never seen so many smart kids have nothing to say. I mean, we were like, "I don't know." "Well, do you think it's money?" We all decided that we definitely didn't think it was money, exactly. That might be a part of it, and that might be some people's dreams; but we decided it was probably success. And that's a hope. And again, the American dream. I mean to have success. To be able to control your destiny almost is the American dream. It's to be able to start over and to be able to work hard to get where you want to get. That's a big deal.

Friday, January 7

This week has not been good at all. I had a test in every single class today. I'd say my biggest problem was being totally bogged down with work this week. I haven't had a lot of free time to do anything.

I'm in my room. It's January 7, 11:30 p.m. The best thing I learned was that I can really, really trust one of my friends. I was talking to him on the computer, and we had the best conversation. And he just listens and understands. It's not like he judges or comments or anything, which is really cool because I can vent to him.

School could be better if it were more relaxed, if I didn't have to do everything right now. Like, if all the tests weren't on the same day, that would be a good thing. It's just that for a while we will be doing nothing, and then we'll be so crazy. That is the part I hate about school. They should spread stuff out more, or something. But the worst part about that is every teacher thinks his or her class is the most important, so you should be doing that first. That's just crappy for them because you just pick what you like, and that's what you spend the most time doing. Period. No one does it any other way.

There are rumors around school about the New Year's parties, and I'm just sick of hearing about it: what everyone did or didn't do and why they're fighting about it. Crazy. And that was my week. So, I'm going to go. Bye.

Sunday, January 9, 8:40 p.m., in my room

My parents are splitting up, and my dad just moved out. I went to my dad's for the first time. It went all right, I guess. We played games, ate spaghetti. Turned out okay.

The best moment of the week? That's difficult. The best moment of the week was Friday night talking to my friend online. I mean, because that just makes my day or my week. We have so much in common when we are connected. It was just great. To know that people are there for you is great. That's the best moment. Definitely. Because you need that. If you don't have friends like that and have people like that in your life, you'll go crazy. You need someone to level you out. It's great.

I'm kinda in a rush today because I have to go baby-sit, and I have to write a paper for my humanities class. It's shocking after this crazy week at school that we have more work (not at all surprising to me). So, I guess I'd better go. Bye.

Sunday, 9:00 p.m.

I'm going to talk about my problems now. One of my big problems right at this moment is my parents' divorce, because I just found out about it not that long ago and my dad just moved out. And, you know, it bothers me not so much because they're splitting up, because that happens all the time, but that I wasn't told there were problems. I didn't see that there were problems. They totally kept them hidden from me, so this was a big shock to me. The thing that bothers me is that my dad immediately moved in with this woman he had been seeing. I think Dad totally sucks. That bothers me a lot. And there's nothing I can do about it, obviously. I just deal with it, which is the best, the only, thing I can do. I think it's hard.

But now I'm going to tell you a great story. Since I was a little kid, all my life, these two people have been like brothers to me. I remember their parents getting divorced when we were little. When they did, I remember my parents telling me that this one friend of mine, Andrew, said, "Does this mean I get two Nintendos?" And after I heard they were getting divorced, I was really upset and told my mom's friend Colleen that I wished I could be like Andrew: just say, "Does this mean I get two Nintendos?" But I'm not. Yesterday when I went to my dad's, the most ironic thing happened. We got there, and he goes, "Oh, well, Donna (the woman he's living with) and I have a Christmas gift for you, an extra Christmas gift for you." So I open it, and it's a Nintendo. I laughed hysterically. I couldn't even believe the irony in that situation. I got my Nintendo. I mean, how sick is that? That's funny. And then I told Colleen, and she was, like, "You're kidding. You're kidding. There's no way he got you a Nintendo." He did. It was so funny. I think that's just an incentive to get us to go there. He's trying to bribe us, I think. He doesn't have to, but, you know, it's something to do when we're there. Hey, I'm not complaining.

If I could change one thing...

I would change people. A person is smart. People are dumb. So true. And people do stupid things: Columbine and all the terrorist acts. I'm glad nothing happened on New Year's. I thought it might. I was a little worried about that.... And I think people need to get less selfish. They have to think about humans, all humanity—not just themselves and what they want to accomplish. And sometimes that's just to hurt people. It's crazy.

The future

In the future, I want to graduate college, to get a good job, to have a nice house and a nice car, to have a family and, obviously, to get married. That, obviously, comes in there after college and stuff. I don't know, like, I just want to be happy. Not that I'm not now, but I mean forever. That's the only thing.

The worst thing that could happen

Try to think of the worst thing that could happen. I think the worst thing that could happen is for someone who means something to you, someone you are just getting to know in your life, is taken from you. That would suck because it is so important to get to know these people. That could screw you up forever. I was just thinking about that because of this girl in my class at school.... There was this hockey camp when we were younger, and she and a bunch of my friends went. She had a heart condition. She was swimming in the pool and she drowned. She died, and everyone at the camp had to be sent home. It was this huge deal, and it still really upsets people who were her friends. That was years and years and years ago. Actually, next year, our senior year, we're going to dedicate our hockey season to her. We should take the division next year because we're that good.

We're going for the championship next year—for her. And, I mean, that's just something that sticks with you forever. It still makes people cry to talk about it, which is, I guess, a growing experience. It can also hurt like hell.

My dad moved out

I used to always eat dinner with my parents every single night—I'm just looking at the survey—but, you know, now my dad moved out, so it's different. It'll be dealt with. That's the thing. Griping about changes isn't going to help. Crying about them isn't going to help. If you don't like the way something is, do something to change it or deal with it. There's nothing I can do to change this. So, I'm just going to deal with it in the best way, the only way, really. What am I gonna do? Throw a hissy fit? Run away? Can I at least hope that's what most people think? Because if they deal with it another way, it's just going to keep coming back. You have to face it. So, that's basically my opinion on that.

Drug and alcohol abuse

Drug and alcohol abuse is a huge problem in my school. The administration tends to ignore it, or to be a part of it, depending on whether the administration is talking about it. But most of the administrators have some problems with drug and alcohol abuse. So, it's kinda hard to stop it at school, isn't it? Occasionally, drug dogs come in and people get suspended; but most people carry their stuff with them, so they wouldn't know. That's just a problem that we need to do something about, if they'll ever admit that there is a problem. It's crazy.

Books and music

For Christmas I got *Harry Potter* books on tape. I like them. They don't say anything deep, but it's really, really interesting and cool writing.… It doesn't have very much to do with anything. I just think the lives and hearts of America could be taught quite a bit by Harry Potter. Just because he's so, like, good hearted in the book, and I like it. It would be a good example for children, I think.

I'm definitely into music. Oh, *Dead Poets' Society,* my favorite movie, has the same message as *Rent.* You know, *No David Today,* that kind of thing. And I don't live by that as much as I think I should. It's hard to. It's hard to remember that all the time. But I do the best I can.

The religion thing

That's a big thing because I'm a nonconformist. A lot of my friends are really religious. And I don't believe in that. I know this is going to sound really weird, but I can't picture worshiping a god in the sense they believe it to be. Because anyone who would put us on a place like this planet to deal with all the stuff we have to go through, to live this life, for what appears to be to us no reason, is not someone I can respect. Or worship. That's just my opinion. Plus, Creation itself is just so far-fetched. I'm sorry, but to me it is. And, in that way, I connect with Zac and Darius. They think the exact same thing. And a lot of my friends don't. It's a big part of who I am, and that's been an obstacle.

Movies

I think now I want to go back to talking about movies because what I think about them is a big deal. *The Breakfast Club* talks about everyone's similarities in the end, and that is something I think people definitely, definitely need to know. Need to see. Need to feel. It's great. As crazy as this is, *Ferris Bueller's Day Off* is one of my all-time favorite movies because, as Ferris says, "Life moves pretty fast. If you don't take time to sit around once in a while, you might miss it." And that's just a message. Important. And I try to remember that. Try to think about that. Try to think about all these things.

And in *The Breakfast Club* and *Dead Poets' Society,* people should see and hear all these things, get the messages, and learn from them. Learn from the story. It's the best thing we can do. I think that's why TV and movies and music are so important. Because I think if you're not using it to get a message across, you're not doing your job (as far as the people who put this stuff together). Sure, you need things that are just fun. I love the movie *Grease*. It doesn't say a lot, but I also think it's important that you use that for good. Use it to teach people a lesson. Just like *Rent,* which might not be a completely true story. But you need to look at this period in history. *Rent* says if you're poor, if you're dying, if you're lonely, you're not alone. Other people are going through exactly the same thing. It says that you can't let it control you. You have to move on. You're still the same person. You have to look at living with disease, not dying from it. You have to learn how not to disconnect from your life, your feelings, your emotions. To really live life, to really be a person, to enjoy it, you need to feel it. Good and bad. You need to experience whatever you can. You need to learn from your mistakes and from the mistakes of others. Then you need to try not to make them again. I told my brother last night that you fall off the horse once, okay. You fall off the horse twice, okay. Get back on. You fall off the third time and it's not the horse; it's the rider. I believe in perseverance, but… That's another thing. You have to know when to give up. You learn it with age, learn it with experience, and I don't think you can speed that up. The more you read about these struggles, or hear about these struggles in history (different things that have gone on), the more prepared you are to deal with your own. It just helps. Helps a lot. I would advise anyone to try to do that. Anyone, young or old; it doesn't matter, because everyone's the same. I think more people need to know that. Just because you're smart doesn't mean sometimes you don't just wanna forget everything, all your problems. Or just because you live in a nice, big house on Main Street, with parents who are always there for you and great siblings and stuff, doesn't mean you're happy. You have to realize everybody has problems. It's just the way you deal with them that classifies you as who you are. I think that's a great thing for humanity—to be able to show all the times when you've persevered; our most human of times, I guess you could say, like when we finally saw the light. That's what all the stories and songs and stuff I like are about. They show me that. We are more than it seems. We're not the masses. Just here. I think you have to help others to be truly happy. I think you have to know others, and I can definitely respect that.

The 411 on My Generation

Jasmine Miller

Kids and Technology

Imagine this. A father is typing a business report on the computer. Suddenly the system goes berserk! It starts deleting files as the astonished dad looks on. He has no idea how to fix his problem and is about to call a computer consultant when his ten-year-old son walks over to the computer and calmly deactivates the system. It immediately resumes normal functions. "My teacher taught me that in second grade," says the boy. "By the way, do we have any bananas?"

Kids are more involved with technology now than they ever were before. For example, my friend has a little brother who can play every computer game they own, including all four "Freddie the Fish" titles and the 3-D chess game his sister got for Christmas. The age of her brother? He's four, and he already has his own computer in his room. And yes, this story is true.

It just goes to show that kids are more involved with computers (as well as with technological baby sitters, such as Nintendo and Game Boys) now, more than ever.

Being Multiethnic

I'm a girl who can hold chopsticks in one hand and a fork in the other. My parents can do the same. I have two New Years in my year: one Chinese and one American. I have my mother's Asian eyes and my father's red-brown hair. My brother is the same. We are multiethnic.

One hundred years ago, this simple introduction would have been quite surprising. No one would ever have imagined that someone was multiethnic. In fact, the word *multiethnic* probably did not exist. These days, being Eurasian is not as unusual as it used to be, but it is still rare. After all, only four percent of the Millennials in the United States are multiethnic. Wait a second, the U.S. census records being multiethnic as a race, right? So, should not all race-evaluative material do the same? I guess not. More than one state I know of does not let you fill in more than one race bubble on school testing papers, but maybe they will change soon.

The Worst Day of My Life

9/11: The worst day of my life, the worst day of my generation's life. Period. Why? Because it changed everything. On that day, we started to grow up. We realized that life was not all fun and games. We realized that, yes, something horrible could happen to us, and, no, America is not immune to danger. Gradually the initial shock wore off and life seemingly returned to normal, but the tragedy was still there, tucked into our memories, changing our lives forever. Though my friends and I did not really talk about 9/11, our social studies book constantly reminded us of it. One page in particular made us upset. It said "America Today" in big bold letters, and underneath it was a picture of the World Trade Center. We avoided that page like the plague.

Parents and Their Kids

As parents and kids get older, they grow farther apart. For example, I am the only girl in my class who goes home and tells her parents what happened in school that day. No one tells their parents their secrets, grudges, crushes, or anything personal at all. Why? I have no idea. The funny thing about it is that people seem to regard me as weird for talking to my mom. Whenever anyone tells me something, they say, "Don't tell your mom," or, "Try not to let your parents know about this." I'm not saying that every kid-parent relationship is horrible or something like that. I'm just saying that the kids that I know are not as close to their parents as they used to be. The best solution to this is simply to spend time with your children. If that does not work, just ask them questions that cannot be answered in one word.

Friends or Not?

What's the deal with friends these days? People will act as if they're best friends with someone and secretly not like them at all! It makes no sense. Relationships are so complicated. You have no way of telling if someone likes you or not. Kids keep too many secrets nowadays. For instance, I know a girl who has grudges against three different girls, but none of them knows about it. Once, one of them found out and the girl pretended to make up with her while telling me about how much she did not like the poor kid. I really do not understand it at all.

Most people think that it is only the girls who are complicated, but the boys are too. I could give you a dozen examples of complex boy relationships right now if I wanted to. Most friends really are true blue, but you can never know.

Kids Are Growing Up Too Fast

Girls don't need to wear Britney Spears outfits at the age of ten, and boys do not need to be all beefed up, either. Don't rush your kids into their teenage years. Childhood is a special time for both parents and children to enjoy. Treasure it while it lasts.

Who Am I?
Second-Generation
Hispanic Americans

Dottie Escobedo-Frank

Growing up as a second-generation American is somewhat like having your feet planted in two different cultures. One foot is firmly placed in the culture of the heart and homeland. It is the culture that draws on the connection to our families. In this connecting place we learn a language of the heart (usually Spanish), a way of thinking and being, and values that are grounded in what it means to be Mexican American, Cuban American, or other designations of the Hispanic population. We grow up grounded in a rich tradition and heritage that forms the heartstrings of our lives.

The second foot is firmly planted in the culture of a homeland. This homeland is where we go to school, develop friendships, learn new values, speak English, and grow proud of the heritage of America. No matter what our backgrounds, a firm foundation is laid as we fully embrace the way of thinking and being called American. In this culture, we hesitate to add on the prefixes of Mexican, Cuban, or Hispanic, because we truly feel no different from the rest of the masses who walk the streets of our lives.

DemoFacts

2000
12.5% of the population is Hispanic.

2020
17% of the population will be Hispanic.

U.S. Bureau of the Census

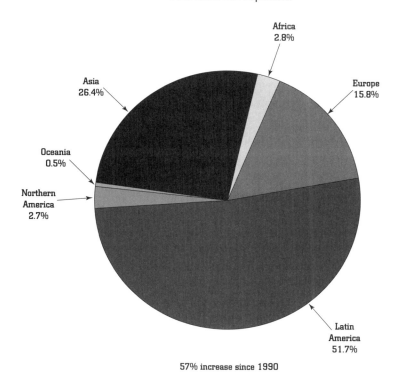

31 Million Foreign-born in 2000

11% of the U.S. Population

Africa 2.8%

Europe 15.8%

Asia 26.4%

Oceania 0.5%

Northern America 2.7%

Latin America 51.7%

57% increase since 1990

Source: U.S. Census Foreign Born by Region of Birth: 2000

Bridging

The word *bridging* is the metaphor I use to describe what is means to grow up as a second-generation American. Bridging recognizes that both cultures—the cultural heritage of our family and the cultural reality of the place where we live—are necessary for our particular understanding of life. Bridging means that we must consider both these points of view to focus clearly on the world. Bridging acknowledges that being grounded in two cultures is like having two strong pillars. The deeper each foundation or pillar, the better the view from the top of the bridge.

Bridging means being able to think, dream, and orient yourself in two different languages. Bridging opens the doors for connecting points that might not have been evident to monocultural people. It provides a broadening of view and expansion of possibilities.

Tension Points

It is not always easy to be in two cultures, though. The tensions sometime bring the strain of being misunderstood. The pull from opposite polarities is extremely difficult.

Religion is one of the places where tensions are strong. For example, while many second-generation Hispanics are Catholic by birth, they may actually attend Protestant churches. However, when there are significant life transition events (baptisms, confirmation, *quinceneras,* marriages, and funerals), extended families will often demand that ceremonies occur in the Catholic Church. Many second-generation Americans deal with this tension by dropping out of both the mother church and their adopted congregation. Also, second-generation people sometimes develop the dominant cultural view on social issues, which may go against the view of the Catholic Church. One learns early to think apart from the church and to question some mores and doctrines.

Language preferences change as second-generation people attend school. Although they have been speaking Spanish in their younger years, a transition occurs when English becomes more comfortable than their birth language. A child's role in the family changes as he or she becomes an interpreter for parents on such important issues as tax letters, drivers' license applications, and notifications by phone of births and deaths. The role of child is cut short when the child interprets adult business and adult situations for his or her parents.

Children's knowledge of a separate language from the language spoken by their parents can also cause strain. Usually, first-generation people (the parents) learn the dominant language of the new culture to some degree, but rarely do they learn to speak and understand the new language as well as their children do. For example, children often read in two languages, while their parents often read in only one. Children may speak in English in front of parents who do not know the language, thereby creating a barrier. Sometimes English may become a code language siblings use to exclude parents.

Learning to deal with the tensions created by living with two cultures, then, is a skill that second-generation people must develop. And they must deal not only with the tensions that are created by their own dual cultures but also with the tensions that sometimes develop within their own family.

Developmental Issues

During the first phase of life, a child bonds to parents with strength and certainty. As with all children, these first years of bonding in a second-generation child's life are centered in only one culture, the culture of his or her parents. But once a child goes to school, the cultural division between the dominant worldview of the culture in which the family lives and parental worldview widens significantly. A child's new view of the world includes a new language, new ways of thinking, new values, and even new stories that define the world. While all children go through natural separation from parents at this stage, second-generation children have a wider dividing space between the home culture and the school culture than do children whose home culture and school culture are the same. Many second-generation children react with quiet withdrawal, separation, and shyness until the new cultural values are fully learned.

Educational differences also serve to estrange families. While a parent may have had to forego education in order to hold a low-paying job to provide housing and sustenance, their children are given the opportunities to finish junior high school, high school, and even college. Each educational advance comes with great pride, but the price to family unity is sometimes disruption. Parents do not feel good enough for their children, and children feel separate because of unshared experiences. When you cannot turn to Mom, Dad, or Tia for advice in career and education, where do you go? Many families bridge these differences and remain close-knit, but the tension still exists.

Race, by Race Alone, 1990 to 2000 Census 2000 PHC-T-1. Population by Race and Hispanic or Latino Origin for the United States: 1990 & 2000			
	1990	**2000**	**Increase**
Other Race	249,093	467,770	87.8%
Hispanic/ Latino	22,354,059	35,305,818	57.9%
Asian	6,642,481	10,123,169	52.4%
Black	29,216,293	33,947,837	16.2%
A. Indian/ N. Alaskan	1,793,773	2,068,883	15.3%
N. Hawaiian/ P. Islander	325,878	353,509	8.5%
White	188,128,296	194,552,774	3.4%

What Your Church Can Do

Go to www.census.gov and then to the 2000 U.S. Census. There you can type in the address of your church and get a demographic profile of your community. As you look at the data, ask these questions:

- Does our church reflect the ethnic diversity of our community?

- Do the children in our community interact with a variety of ethnic groups?

- Does our congregation match up with the age groupings in the community?

- What changes do we need to make to reflect the people who now live in our community?

Use *NextChurch.Now: Creating New Faith Communities,* by Craig Kennet Miller, as a study with key leaders in your congregation to create a vision for reaching new people groups in your community.

Millennial Multiethnic View Versus Dominant Monoethnic View

Multiethnic Millennial children grow up knowing a world that is truly diverse. In school, they see many skin variations, hear many languages, and experience many religious celebrations. Variety, not singularity, is the norm. Second-generation children live out diversity in every part of their lives. While the older generations still operate in a single-ethnic manner, these children may think it is odd to be in a group consisting of only one type of people.

For the second-generation Hispanic, this multiethnic view is liberating. While older generations may inflict some racism in their direction, their peers do not. This acceptance factor provides a way for a bridging person to be accepted and valued.

Ministry With Second-Generation Millennials

Ministry with second-generation Millennials needs to be inclusive, bicultural, and grounded in a faith that makes sense in their everyday lives. Now, more than ever, the church must open its doors and find ways to be truly multiethnic and inclusive. If we remain one color, one view, and one manner, we will have difficulty bringing the gospel to the next generation. Many people are convinced that the only way to be the church is to sit in the pew next to people just like us. But the Millennial Generation will not sit in pews that exclude their best friends. We must move on the journey of inclusive, multiethnic ministry in order to reach second-generation Millennials.

To be bicultural is a broader issue. A bicultural church finds ways to minister to first-, second-, and third-generation people as well as to those people who span two cultures. Families may be made up of varied races and cultures. Parents may experience a culture different than the culture of their children. Families are hoping to go to a church that has a ministry that grandma, mom, and child can work in together. To accomplish this, some churches may have services in English, in Spanish, or in a combination of languages.

Faith must make sense for every person's life. With such a broad scope of experience in everyday life, second-generation people are seeking a faith that is dynamic, changing, grounded, and growing. Scripture must be learned in new, exciting, and basic ways. Technology and creative arts will reach this generation in the same way that previous generations were moved by rich organ music. Multifaceted, fast-paced worship services will make sense and speak the gospel in a way that touches bridging people.

What Your Church Can Do

1. Develop multiethnic staffing patterns. Begin inclusivity now to prepare for the future.

2. Develop multigenerational ministries that cross barriers of style and preference. Teach valuing of the "other."

3. Learn a new language and practice it. Reach out to the unfamiliar in your community.

4. Learn Latin, Asian, and other musical tempos. Grow in understanding and appreciation for new sounds.

5. Put second-generation laity in key leadership positions. They will then help shape the church of the future.

Youth and Their Music

Chris Hughes

Music is well said to be the speech of angels; in fact, nothing among the utterances allowed to man is felt to be so divine. It brings us near to the infinite.

(Thomas Carlyle, 1795–1881)

*T*he *Faith We Sing* is an apt title for the songbook published by The United Methodist Publishing House. That title perhaps has even more truth in it than may have been intended by the editors. What we sing and the music we know by heart—our oldies from the formerly well-defined realms of the secular and the sacred—shape our worldview and our theology. Both the pop songs and the church music from your adolescence have shaped your soul and trigger in you potent memories, beliefs, and feelings.

The same thing is happening with youth today. If you ask churched teens what music is sacred to them, they will first try to give the answer they think you are looking for: "Christian music." However, most teens, even Christian teens, do not buy or listen to a lot of Christian music. You can help them by asking the right questions: "What music do you listen to, especially in private? What music feeds your soul?" The culture has blurred the lines between sacred and secular. But life is life. Any music from any source that speaks to me is my sacred music.

Mix is the operative word in homemade collections of personal music—and it may seem to you like an odd mix. Rap, hip-hop, classic rock, pop, and blues may all end up in the same teen's CD collection. Our foster son, Doug (an African-American teen), listened to urban rap with his friends as well as to the soundtrack from *The Lion King.*

Adolescence is a time when identity is in flux. In fact, identity formation goes hand in hand with faith formation as the central task of adolescence. Adolescence is the critical time for asking, "Who am I?" and "Who am I in relationship with God in Jesus Christ and the Christ community?" Music is so much a part of youth culture and so powerful a faith-forming influence that you simply must plug in!

Hard-Wired for Musical Encounters With God

Recent studies in brain science and neurobiology confirm that we are hard-wired for experiences of God, and that music and rhythm are key elements in those experiences.[1] Whether it comes through slow, rhythmic, repetitive, meditative music or through fast, energetic beat and movement, the boundaries between the self, others, and the world outside are blurred in spiritual experiences. We experience unity with

DemoFacts

- Forty-six percent of teens selected listening to music, twenty percent selected listening to the radio, and nineteen percent selected playing music when asked the three ways they most often spend their free time.

- Forty-seven percent of teens carry a CD player with them.

- Eighty-five percent of teens surveyed have Internet access in their home, and twenty-four percent said surfing the Net is one of three ways they most often spend their free time.

- Only eleven percent of teens picked Christian music (including inspirational, contemporary, and gospel) as one of their two favorite kinds of music.

Millennium Generation Survey, 2002

others in worship and with God. These experiences are perceived as spiritual unions, whether it is the satisfying sense of a congregation coming together in the closing harmonious strains of a hymn or a moment of mystical union with Christ in communion or in meditation. Music is a sure path to encounters with God.

The Search for *We* and *Me*

Youth are on a search for both community and self, for both belonging and standing out, for both the *we* and the *me.* All of the music we choose to listen to feeds a tribal identity: "My friends and I listen to this (and not to that)." Music also feeds a private, developing soul identity. Some music you listen to in a social context you would not necessarily choose in a more private context. Some of your private stock you may not want to play in a group setting.

Music is a part of identity building. Youth identify with certain kinds of music and artists, and those music styles and artists identify youth. We would do well to point young people to music that shapes Christian identity, including the self as one for whom Christ dies and lives and as one who is called to continue the ministry of Jesus in the world. It is an identity rooted in the Christian community, both *my* church and *the* church, the body of Christ in the world.

Moving Beyond Gate-Keeping to Developing Discernment Skills

Music-sharing technology, including MP3 players, home-burnt CDs, and the ready availability on the Internet of virtually all kinds of music, presents a real challenge to gate-keeping and protective modes of youth ministry (which never worked, anyway). Better to educate yourself and explore the territory with teens than to make vain and counterproductive attempts to block, ignore, or condemn the music youth listen to. Prepare yourself and youth peer leaders to navigate the musical landscape and converse more fluently in a variety of musical languages.

Youth have a decidedly more relaxed attitude toward the twin pillars of adult measures of decency: crude language and expressions of sexuality. However, seeking to understand and establish dialogue is not the same as condoning harsh, crude, and demeaning words and images. Together, teens and adults can develop the practice of choosing and consciously reflecting on music.

Our Sacred Music

Culture has blurred the lines between sacred and secular. What, then, makes music sacred? We have described sacred music as music that feeds the soul. Any music that speaks to me is my sacred music. How might we help Millennials evaluate their sacred music?

S Is for Source and Story

One definition of the word *source* deals with origin, the thing from which something is derived. Look at Luke 6:43-45. What kind of roots and trees produce a song's emotional and lyric content? Read Numbers 21:16-18. What "springs up" in the song and in you as you listen to it? That water gives a clue to the digger of the well.

Millennial Voices

The people I hang out with listen to a lot of heavy music that I would never listen to (by myself).

Sarah, age 15

Millennial Voices

When I listen to rock 'n' roll Christian music and stuff, [my dad says,] "That's not religious music… It's got to be slow…it can't have drums."

Kris, age 17

A second definition of *source* points to somebody or something providing information, opinions, or evidence. We need reliable sources. Is your source reliable? How do you know? Where do you get information about yourself, your world, others? Start with Psalm 139:1-18. Then look at Psalm 8 and 1 Peter 2:9-10. Who are you going to believe?

A third definition of *source* relates to the creative arts. A source is a work on which another work is based. Ask, "What works are reinforced, encouraged, and inspired by my music?"

Finally, from the realm of geography, a *source* is the spring or fountain from which a river or stream first issues from the ground. In Proverbs 5:15, we are encouraged to "drink water from [our] own cistern, flowing water from [our] own well." Is your music a source of living water or of poisoned water? In Matthew 12:33-37, Jesus says, "Out of the abundance of the heart the mouth speaks." What music fills and feeds your heart?

S is also for story. How does the music you listen to help you tell your own life story? Do you connect your situation to the story and the feelings in your music? Our story is the story of God's people, and we join our story with the story of Jesus and the followers of Jesus.

A Is for Attitude

What is the attitude of both the music and the performers? What attitudes are expressed by the video or other visual images connected with the song? Read 1 Corinthians 13:4-8, substituting the phrase *my music* for the word *love.*

C Is for Content

Words matter. Youth and adults have different tolerance levels for street language. Even though sound and beat are foremost attractors, teens affirm that words matter—or, more accurately, meaning matters. Meaning is not just an adult issue; however, the perspectives of youth and adults are often different. Consider the invitation in Philippians 4:8: "Finally, beloved, whatever is true, whatever is honorable, whatever is just, whatever is pure, whatever is pleasing, whatever is commendable, if there is any excellence and if there is anything worthy of praise, think about these things."

R Is for Response

- What is my emotional response? (Music tends to magnify our feelings: joy, depression, anger, peace.)
- What is my physiological response? (What happens to my heart rate and my breathing?)
- What is my mood response? (What mood am I in when I pick a song or CD? What is my mood when I am finished listening?)
- What is my kinetic response? (Do I start to tap my foot, move my head, dance, or stop dead still?)
- Do I have an experience of God? (Read Galatians 5:22. What is the fruit of music in my life?)

E Is for Edification

Read 1 Corinthians 10:23–11:1. Does my music build up people and encourage them? Does it encourage me? Is it good for the people around me? What does it lift up, glorify, celebrate, or proclaim?

DemoFacts

What are your favorite kinds of music? (pick 2)

58% Pop/Rock
53% Rap/Hip-Hop
21% Alternative
18% Soul/Rhythm & Blues
17% Country
11% Contemporary Inspirational/ Christian/Contemporary Christian/ Gospel
10% Classical
5% Latin
3% Metal/Classic Rock/Heavy Metal/ Punk/Techno
4% Other

Millennial Generation Survey, 2002

Millennial Voices

Sometimes the lyrics have a deep meaning. The words matter. The music added to the words makes it even more powerful.

Kris, age 17

Millennial teens are tired of the attitude that everything and everyone "sucks," but they are not suckers for "everything is beautiful," either.

D Is for Defining

How does my music define who I am? Compare and contrast your public and private music listening habits. In ways that count, we become what we pay attention to. The same principle applies to worship music. We become what we adore.

M Is for Memory and Meaning

What memories does your music trigger? Does it remind you of God's grace and mercy? Or does it drag you into guilt or hopelessness? Make music a holy remembrance of healing, joy, peace, and calling to faithful discipleship. Hear the words of Jesus as you listen to your sacred music: "Do this in remembrance of me" (Luke 22:19).

The great thing about great music (and any great art) is that its meaning is mostly up to you, the beholder. Practice hearing God in unlikely music. Let the Holy Spirit break through your compartments of sacred and secular.

U Is for Use

When, where, and for what purpose is my music played? Does it matter? Some teens will be reluctant to play certain music in church settings because of the reputation or stereotype associated with the artist, group, or type of music. Some will want to make relative decisions about the use of some music based on their location, who they are with, or the occasion.

Many adults advocate a right-and-wrong system but model a relative morality that is fraught with hypocrisy and compartmentalized living. Youth have seen adults model the idea that it is all right to do certain things, at certain times, in certain places. Both groups—adults and teens—have their hypocrites and Pharisees. Sometimes the transformation comes in the honest struggle for integrity.

S Is for Spiritual

One definition of *spiritual* is anything that brings or breathes life. Does your sacred music bring life, joy, hope, and peace? If there is anger, is it righteous and for the sake of others? If there is rebellion, is it against injustice? What kind of spirit is present in my music?

I Is for Identity and Image

I see me in my music. I hear my best hopes and my worst fears. What is our identity in the world? It is the one called by the name of Christ. It is Christ-person in a Christ-body-community. Does this identification with Christ and identity in Christ come in part through my music? Do I have to listen only to Christian music to be identified as a Christian? Or, is it my response to and interpretation of the music that identifies me as a disciple of Jesus?

I is also for image. Music is no longer only about sound. Visual images, videos, and musical metaphors form another dimension to seeing music. It is impossible to unsee something. What images come to mind as I consume my sacred music?

Millennial Voices

We tried youth choir two or three times in the last few weeks, and they may sing two or three times and then everybody quits because they don't want to sing out of the hymnal. They want something that's upbeat, something that they listen to, something they relate to—youth music.

Kris, age 17

C Is for Christ-Like and Connective

Do I hear with Jesus' ears? Do I hear and see Jesus' way, wisdom, and character? My friend J. Michael Bryan, who is a minister of worship and a musician, wrote a song called "I Hear Jesus in Your Song." It is a great compliment and something to aspire to.

Music also connects: It connects people to a group. It connects people to story, memory, and emotion. Sacred music connects people to God and to one another under God.

Music Ministry

Music should never be harmful to the hearts and minds of youth; nor should it be throwaway or inconsequential, especially the music embraced by disciples of Jesus. In the same way, the gospel should never be offered as harmless. The gospel challenges as well as comforts. It brings peace and a sword. It exposes the self-interest of religious leaders and institutions. It highlights the needs of those on the edges of life and advocates for faithful responses. It confirms and challenges the best and worst in us. Just so, offer music that is neither bland nor uninspired. Share music that inspires, professes, soothes, incites, heals, exposes, involves, and advocates.

Pointers for Parents and Leaders

- Get real: listen, talk, and respond to (instead of reacting to) what young people are plugged into. Avoid *ought* and *should* judgment calls based on your perspective (not theirs). Instead, be honest and straightforward about your questions, responses, and beliefs.

- Encourage youth to use their heads for something besides a place for headphones to rest. Join them for discernment exercises for "faith-full" listening.

- Contrast ambient music and music in worship, fellowship, and teaching with times of silence and solitude. Help Millennial youth "be still, and know…God" (Psalm 46:10). The highest contrast is not between loud and soft music but between music and no music.

- Use free expression in writing (journals, poetry, autobiographical episodes, personification of sounds or instruments), visual arts, and movement to reveal what music shapes young souls.

- Engage music technology in creative ways. Get young people to teach you about MP3s, mix-n-match CD burning, music in worship using projection, Powerpoint and successive graphic technologies, digital cameras (still images and video), and homegrown music distributed on CD (music evangelism).

- Make connections between young people's music and their lives. It communicates that you care enough to know something about their world. Model a response to their music that they can learn to do for themselves.

- Draw lines from young people's music to Bible stories, characters, and teachings. It means that you will have to become more literate in both the Bible and youth music.

- Explore the images associated with songs and music styles through performing arts and use of visuals: tableaux/silent dramas suggested

Millennial Voices

I'll listen to Christian music; but people think just because of what I look like, I don't listen to that kind of stuff and that I worship the devil or something. But I don't care; I know who I am.

Sarah, age 15

What Your Church Can Do

- Do not make young people be like you before they can be like Jesus.

- Help youth find their voice to worship God and communicate the passion and the content of their faith in their own musical languages and styles. Start and mentor a youth worship team.

- Make every Sunday Youth Sunday in the ways that every Sunday is Children's Sunday and (mostly) Adult Sunday. Incorporate images and lyrics from youth music in sermons, prayers, and liturgies. Use youth sacred music in congregational worship.

Millennial Voices

Dear Mom and Dad,

Thank you so much for something I could only dream of playing, my guitar.... Holding my guitar makes me feel a whole lot better than holding a Nintendo controller in my hands. My first song will be about my parents and how much they love me to give me something my heart desires.... You've made me feel a whole lot better to have control of a musical instrument.

Dayton, age 12,
in a thank-you
note to his parents

by song lyrics, video loops (created by group members or downloaded from the Internet), slide shows using digital pictures and visuals from image banks on the Internet.

- Connect youth to multicultural and cross-tribal styles. Help them out of their narrow tribal musical identities by inviting sharing of their private collection of music and by exposing them to other forms of sacred music.

- Feed youth both public and private Christ-identity-building music:
  — Give young people CDs and custom mixes of sacred music tuned to their ears.
  — Offer the best of secular spiritual/values music. Feed the positive, hopeful, and constructive instincts of Millennial teens.
  — Point them to the best sacred music you can find from both secular and Christian sources.
  — Share with them your sacred music: the music that shaped, and continues to shape, your faith. Invite them to contribute to the mix. Help them offer their sacred music to you, to the church, and to their peers.

- Cultivate music-to-life-to-Bible teaching moments:
  — Explore crossover between secular and sacred music, especially the spiritual nature of *my* music.
  — Explore identity and integrity issues in music.
  — Use music as an entrée to the Scriptures and the traditions and teachings of the church.

- Encourage playing of instruments and singing—making, not just consuming, music.

- Teach music theory. Cultivate combos, bands, ensembles, and choirs, drawing on school bands and garage bands for instrumentation and players.

- Reshape and reposition youth choir as a youth worship team:
  — Move beyond performance for proud parents to worship engagement with the congregation and with unchurched people and youth peers.
  — Incorporate all visual and performing arts, including dynamic unison signing, elements of stomp and step, and other forms of rhythmic speech and hybrid music forms.

Endnote

1 Andrew Newberg and Eugene D'Aquili document in their book *Why God Won't Go Away: Brain Science and the Biology of Belief* (New York: Ballantine Books, 2001) the neurobiological processes of spiritual experience.

Dialogue for a Healthy Sexuality: The Church's Unique Opportunity

James H. Ritchie, Jr.

Parents and professionals who observe youth culture and care about young people are aware of how overexposed today's young people are to sexual imagery. You have seen it, for it is everywhere. In our market-driven culture, someone with a sexual agenda waits around every corner to sell something to our sons and daughters—and to us.

At times, the sexual sales pitch is blatant: You cannot help but be sexy in our jeans. At other times, the pitch takes the subtle approach, relying on gender stereotyping to make the sale. They project a picture of the real boy or the ideal girl feeding on, dressed in, or entertained by their product. Their customer base of insecure preadolescents and teens simply want to fit in with their peers, a diverse peer group with this in common: the fear of being excluded and the desire to be finished growing up. Show them how your product can dispel their fears and fulfill their desires, and watch your market share increase.

I have been both filled with joy and frustrated during the fifteen years I have been developing human sexuality education resources and leading church-based weekend workshops for preteens and their parents.

The joy: seeing parents and children benefit from a greater and earlier access to information regarding sexuality than we Boomers ever knew. We celebrate the increased attention to sexuality-related issues in schools, healthcare organizations, and some congregations.

The frustration: realizing that this enlightenment can neither keep pace with the avalanche of questions that young people are either asking or wanting to ask in response to all they are being exposed to nor counteract what appears to be the resurrection of gender-related stereotypes.

Yes, the media and advertising industries, using stereotypes to capitalize on male and female insecurity, generate many of the questions that young people are asking. But they have help—lots of it. They share culpability with a culture so diverse and with family systems so complex that few questions—beyond those grounded in basic anatomy, physiology, and reproduction—can be answered easily.

We live with diversity. Values related to sexuality and sexual behaviors that we hold personally may not be shared with neighbors whose ethnic, religious, economic, ethical, and cultural backgrounds differ from ours. For that matter, it is not even difficult to find divergent values within families. Issues of right and wrong or appropriate and inappropriate, once readily dispatched with a long-held family, community, or congregational cliché, now resist easy responses. Chances are that someone holding contrasting (even opposing) values lives right next door, works in the adjacent cubicle, or sits at the other

DemoFacts

The percentage of students who ever had sexual intercourse decreased from fifty-four percent to forty-six percent from 1991 to 2001, and those who had four or more sexual partners decreased from nineteen percent to fourteen percent. Simultaneously, the percentage of sexually active students who used a condom at last sexual intercourse increased from 1991 to 1999 (forty-six percent to fifty-eight percent) and then leveled by 2001 (fifty-eight percent).

Centers for Disease Control and Prevention press release; June 27, 2002

end of your pew. So, the pile of unanswered or unsatisfactorily answered questions grows and grows.

Many of the Millennials I work with each year show relatively little willingness to separate themselves from resurging gender stereotypes. One of the learning activities in the *Created by God* study I lead with fifth and sixth graders and their parents calls for the young people to create montages from pictures and words torn or clipped from the pages of magazines. One montage depicts their impressions of what it means to be female, and the other what it means to be male. I almost feel guilty using this activity, as though I'm setting the group up for my preprogrammed attack on the stereotypes they continue to buy into. We Baby Boomers like to believe that our generation inflicted lethal damage on gender-related stereotypes.

To the credit of the Boomer Generation, society is now slower to restrict occupations to a single gender. Women find greater acceptance as community and corporate leaders. Men are allowed some latitude when it comes to demonstrating sensitivity. In some arenas, the term *humankind* has replaced *mankind;* and when we make reference to all people, we do not assume that the words *all men* generate mental pictures of both genders.

But these victories have proven less conclusive than that of Joshua before the walls of Jericho. The Baby Boomers' trumpets have grown quiet, interest has waned, and the stereotypes appear to be returning with a renewed vigor. Why? Could it be that these stereotypes, whether or not we agree with them, provide something definitive, something conclusive, that young people are not finding elsewhere— not even in our theologically and socially sound sexuality education experiences? Young people are searching for the bottom line, for a sense of closure: This is what it means to be male. This is what it means to be female. This is how males and females are expected to interact. These are acceptable behaviors; those are not.

It is interesting how the agenda of the media and the advertising industry so closely parallels that of church and parachurch organizations calling for a return to traditional values. Men are men, women are women, and sex is forbidden outside of marriage. Just say no. Trying to market their products, advertisers often sound like evangelists, and evangelists often sound like marketing specialists. While advertisers woo our children to just say yes, and those advocating traditional values woo them to just say no, wooing is wooing, and our daughters and sons need help with their responses.

Even those most supportive of the just-say-no approach must admit that it takes a lot of no's to fill the space between puberty and marriage. We live with the reality that the gap between the onset of puberty and the taking of marriage vows shows no sign of decreasing. Similarly, the gap between the onset of puberty and first sexual experience shows no sign of increasing. Add to this the fact that nearly a third of the Millennials have been born to unmarried parents. Over a third will experience the divorce of their parents by the time they are 18. These facts introduce the phenomenon of parental dating and a young person having to simultaneously make sense of parental sexuality and his or her own.

Now factor in the exposure to ethnic, cultural, ethical, and moral diversity on the topic of sexuality and sexual behaviors, and it is no wonder that confused young people will ultimately rely on sexual stereotypes when they are choosing what to wear, deciding how to spend their free time, and making decisions regarding sexual involvement. Nothing new about that approach. Brains put on hold, bodies lead the dance. If no one can tell me the difference between right and wrong, I will just do what feels right.

Some Christian people demand strong, unwavering position statements from the church—statements that clearly define acceptable behavior, and by virtue of that behavior, who stands inside and who stands outside the circle of faith. Given the diversity with which we live, it is no wonder that a cry has sounded for this kind of clarity. But with such clear definitions comes the potential for stereotyping and for the dismissal of grace and tolerance. Should we be teaching our children that sexuality has become the primary test for determining who is welcome and who is unwelcome in our congregations?

Perhaps the strong position needed is one that would call for creating and supporting settings in the church for dialogue on the subject of sexual attitudes and behaviors. Where one set of parents might not be able to oppose the media/advertising monster, a dialogue-inspired coalition of parents might. Divorced parents reentering the dating world—sometimes at the same time their children are entering it for the first time—might benefit from the experience of others who have walked that path, or from the support of others making their way through it. Some parents are perfectly comfortable talking about issues related to sexuality with their children, and others—despite progress made in the past few decades—are frightened to death with the idea. Here the church could make a firm commitment to providing an arena where parents and children can come together to learn, to practice using a new vocabulary, and to discover the seldom-recognized intimate link between spirituality and sexuality.

From my perspective, the satisfaction of involvement in human sexuality education comes at the end of an event as I watch the parents and young people depart side by side. Parents look as though the weight of the world has been lifted from their shoulders. They return home feeling as though they are not alone in the task of building a solid foundation for a healthy approach to human sexuality. They have talked with other adults, with their children, and with other people's children about subjects they have never talked about before, using language they seldom get to use. They sense that the whole church stands behind them and walks beside them.

The sons and daughters of these newly liberated parents depart with the confidence that they know everything there is to know about bodies, growth and development, responsible behaviors, where babies come from, sexual abuse, and what it means to have been created a sexual being by God. However, reality will set in; and when it does, they will have in place print resources, parents, and other caring adults in the church to stimulate, correct, or supplement their memories. Even if they do not retain every term and every definition, they leave

Pointers for Parents

Schedule an opportunity for a group of parents (perhaps an established Sunday school class or study group or the parents of young people involved in a church fellowship group) to discuss questions such as these:

- What questions are your sons and daughters asking, and what issues are you having to deal with related to sexuality?

- How are you, as parents, responding, or how might you respond within the family?

- How can the church become a more active part of this conversation?

What Your Church Can Do

Review available resources for group study of human sexuality; then bring one or more proposals to the church's program leadership body for initiating structured opportunities for dialogue. Keep parents involved and/or informed at every step of the decision-making process.

with the knowledge that they have been respected and listened to by those who have dared to talk with them about adult matters.

We have to talk—young people with young people, parents with parents, parents with their own children and with someone else's children. We cannot build walls high enough to prevent our children from having contact with views and values that differ from ours. Healthy understandings of sexuality will not be achieved apart from our dialogue together. In the midst of our great diversity, we must search together for answers to the questions that our children are asking. As we search, let us celebrate the God who created us sexual and who, in the Spirit of Christ, stands with us and guides us and our children in that search.

The Battle for the Hearts and Souls of Preteens

Craig Kennet Miller

What do Harry Potter, the Disney Channel, and confirmation have in common? They all are targeted to our newest demographic group on the block, the preteens (ages eight to fourteen).

Why are preteens so important? Because as children become preteens, they begin to make their own decisions separate from their parents. It is during this time that events and experiences begin to shape values and beliefs that will last a lifetime.

When an eight-year-old goes to the mall with a friend for the first time, what will he or she buy? This is the question that keeps CEOs of companies such as Nike, Coca-Cola, and The Gap up late at night.

The power of preteens' choices can be seen in the results of the 2001 summer movie season. The number-one movie, with sales of more than 267 million dollars, was *Shrek.* Squarely aimed at preteens and their parents, *Shrek* took great delight in skewing everything Disney. In one scene as the princess sings to a bluebird, you are reminded of scenes from such Disney classics as *Cinderella* and *Snow White,* where the animals join the main characters in song and mirth. In *Shrek,* though, the princess's voice becomes so shrill that the bird explodes. In the next scene, the princess is seen cooking the eggs the bird left behind in her nest. This irrelevant romp through the world of fairy tales fits the mindset of preteens, who are in that never-never land between childhood and adolescence.

What is unique about preteens is that they are at the heart of the emerging Millennial culture, which will find full flower in 2006. Unlike their predecessors, they will come into adolescence and adulthood equipped with tools and information never seen by any previous generation.

Techno-Kids

Born in the 1990's, today's preteens do not know a world without computers, the Internet, cable TV, DVDs, Game Boys, and the X-Games. Their sources of information range from books, magazines, parents, and friends to the wide range of electronic information devices available in virtually every shape and form. As a result, today's preteen literally processes information differently from our oldest generations. Most seventy-year-olds would have great difficulty watching a music video on MTV because they would not be able to process the rapid images that a preteen can in a blink of an eye. Or, put a forty-year-old next to a preteen on the latest video game console, and who do you think will win?

Pointers for Parents

Is your child more likely to play football outside or in front of a screen? With your child, determine how much time per week he or she is spending in front of the TV, computer, and video game console. Ask the following:

• How much time do you think you should spend in front of a screen?

• If you cut back, how else could you use that time?

• What are you learning from your favorite TV show or video game?

• Does the entertainment option share your values?

Preteen Millennials have been exposed to many things early in life, so what may seem new and exciting to adults may be old hat to Millennials. However, today's preteens may not be smarter than previous generations. If a church thinks having a PowerPoint presentation during worship will attract Millennials, they may be operating on the wrong assumption. Today's fourth graders are learning how to do PowerPoint at school. Having PowerPoint at church may be new to adults, but for preteens it is just another communication device. Whether to use PowerPoint at church brings up a much larger question of what the church has to offer. As we will see, the church is not the only one asking what they have to offer to kids today.

Kids as a Market

Blame it on Disney if you want. In the late 1980's, Disney embarked on a strategy of creating a new series of characters that kids would love just as much as they loved Mickey Mouse. So, starting in 1989, Disney released a series of new animated films. The first wave of Millennials grew up to the sights and sounds of *The Little Mermaid* (1989), *Beauty and the Beast* (1991), *Aladdin* (1992), and *The Lion King* (1994). Just as Baby Boomers know *The Wizard of Oz* by heart, Millennials can sing all the songs from these movies.

By the time *Pocahontas* was released in the summer of 1995, Disney had a well-oiled marketing machine in place. But Disney's strategy moved beyond making a movie. Instead, its goal was the sale of toys, CDs, videos, storybooks, CD-ROMs, and figurines given out at fast-food restaurants. *Beauty and the Beast* and *The Lion King* even became Broadway musicals. For *Pocahontas,* major corporations spent 125 million dollars for a record number of tie-in merchandise. Disney alone produced forty different picture and activity books, not to mention icons of the movies being placed on backpacks, lunch boxes, shoes, and T-shirts. By 1995, just about every elementary school child had at least one Disney character on his or her backpack as he or she trudged off to school each day.

Disney's genius was its ability to capitalize on the sales of videotapes, which allowed parents to show Disney movies on their VCRs at home. Rather than let children watch what was on TV, parents now were the programmers of their children's entertainment; and Disney animated films were at the top of the list. It would not be unusual for a Millennial child to have watched *Beauty and the Beast* and *The Lion King* more than a hundred times before his or her tenth birthday.

Synergy Plus

By 2001, Disney was not the only player in town. In fact, the synergy of Scholastic Inc. and AOL Time Warner produced the biggest mega-hit of them all when their forces combined to produce the marketing phenomena known as *Harry Potter.*

Harry Potter and the Sorcerer's Stone was the first in a series of children's books by J.K. Rowling, a previously unknown British writer. After the release of the first book in 1997, it soon was a hit in Britain. By 1998, it had traveled to America and was published by

Disney's Cable and TV Holdings
(Full and partial ownership)

ESPN
Lifetime
A&E
ESPN2
The History Channel
E! Entertainment
Disney Channel
ESPN Classic
Toon Disney
ESPNEWS
Lifetime Movie Channel
Style
SoapNet
Biography
ABC Family

Scholastic Inc., which advertises itself as the two-billion-dollar publisher of children's books with direct access to thirty-two million children, forty-five million parents, and nearly every school in the United States. Through its onsite book fairs and direct-mail flyers distributed in schools, it holds a position even Disney would envy. Scholastic sells directly to teachers and students alike. Combine a fascinating story line with a great distribution network, and you produce something never seen before, a children's book series that has dominated the New York Times Book Review list since 1998. But the story does not stop there.

Next, add the largest media company ever formed when AOL bought Time Warner. The combined resources of AOL Time Warner include the Warner Brothers movie studio; cable TV properties, such as TBS Superstation, Turner Network Television, Cartoon Network, HBO, CNN, CNN Headline News; and network TV, such as The WB Television Network and Kids' WB! Print media includes *Time, People, Teen People, Sports Illustrated, Entertainment Weekly,* plus many more. Then you add AOL, by far the largest presence on the Internet, and you have the opportunity to market a movie like no one has ever done before.

When Warner Brothers bought the rights for *Harry Potter* in 1997 for 500,000 dollars, little did it know how much this investment would pay off. Even though the first movie cost 125 million dollars to make, that is nothing when you stop to realize that Coca-Cola paid 150 million dollars for the exclusive rights to promote the film and its sequels. With a total of seven movies planned, each rolling out seven years in a row, it is estimated that total sales of movie ticket, video, music, and merchandise sales will come to more than ten billion dollars in gross revenue and two billion dollars in profit.

But synergy does raise some questions. When *Time* magazine had an exclusive look at the finished film, its film critics did not see the movie. Instead, the preview story was written by one of the magazine's entertainment reporters, whose quotes were used as a critic's blurb in the studio's opening-weekend print ads. As one studio executive admitted, this was one franchise they did not want to mess up.

Attention Getters

Preteen Millennials have garnered the attention of corporations because of one simple fact: They spend close to fourteen billion dollars a year, not to mention the influence they have on the purchases made by their parents. Because preteens have all their potential purchases ahead of them, companies see them as the ultimate source of job security. Get them while they are young, and they will stay with you through their adult years.

Everyone from sports teams to clothing manufacturers are trying to figure out how to get their share of the pie. The revealing book *Sole Influence: Basketball, Corporate Greed, and the Corruption of America's Youth,* by Dan Wetzel and Don Yaeger, tells the story of how Nike and Adidas fight it out on the nation's playgrounds to find the next Michael Jordan. By sponsoring summer basketball camps and inviting

DemoFacts

The *Harry Potter* movies, music, and merchandise are estimated to generate more than ten billion dollars for AOL Time Warner.

Pointers for Parents

Parents are responsible for setting the boundaries for entertainment options. Rather than placing TVs, DVDs, and Internet connections in the child's bedroom, it is better to create an entertainment and information room or space where all members of the family have access. This allows easy monitoring of TV programs or Internet choices and offers opportunities to dialogue and learn together.

top fourteen-year-old prospects, shoe companies hope to gain top players' trust and loyalty. When it is time to sign that multi-million-dollar shoe contract, they hope the newest NBA stars will remember how well they were taken care of when they were young. When these players make their first slam dunks, shoe corporations want to make sure it is their logo that will be seen.

Thus, soon after signing with the Lakers in 1996 right out of high school, Kobe Bryant signed a five-year, multi-million-dollar deal with Adidas. Sonny Vaccaro, an employee of Adidas, had discovered Bryant during the previous two summers, when Bryant had attended basketball camps run by Vaccaro that were aimed at discovering new talent. Vaccaro's earlier claim to fame was signing Michael Jordan in 1984 for an endorsement deal with Nike.

How Does the Church Compete?

Churches know that the battle for the attention of today's preteens is fierce. Talk to most pastors and you will hear them bemoan the fact that instead of coming to worship, preteens are playing hockey, soccer, basketball, football, and baseball. Or, even more puzzling, they are doing something called extreme sports. Add to that homework, music lessons, dance lessons, and so forth, and today's generation of preteens seems to have little time for church.

Which brings us back to the question, What does the church have to offer to preteens? The reality is that the church cannot outentertain Disney. But it can outrelationship them. For the Millennials, like every generation that has come before, the quality of the relationships they have with their friends and family is what is most important.

While parents may think that what they need to offer is the latest gadget, what makes the most difference is time to talk and to relate. Patricia Hersch, in her book *A Tribe Apart: A Journey Into the Heart of American Adolescence*, points out that kids do the best when they have a strong family supporting them and are involved in relationships and activities.

The goal for churches is not to make Millennials into church members but to create a web of relationships that witnesses to them the reality of a God who loves them. You will capture their attention not by offering the newest thing but by making the old, old story of Jesus and his love new to them. Each believer can point to a time when Jesus' story spoke to him or her. What children and youth long for are adults who will take the time to make the story real.

The battle for the souls of preteens is a reality. The choice a congregation makes about its relationship to children, youth, and young adults in their church and in their community is an eternal one. Each congregation must ask if it is willing to make the sacrifices in time and energy it takes to share its faith with this new generation. Who knows, maybe in the process they will be born again to the joy of being in the presence of those who find out that there is a place for them in God's family.

What Your Church Can Do

Rather than ignore the latest mega-movie or best-selling children's book, make sure you see it or read it. Pastors and leaders can redeem the culture by finding elements of a movie or book that echo the gospel story and using it in preaching. Also, do not be afraid to ask questions or to challenge children, youth, and parents about what values they find in their entertainment options. Does having six channels of HBO in the home create a child-friendly environment? Does the latest first-person video game whose main character's goal is to kill everything affect a person's tolerance of violence? By asking questions, the church can help children, youth, and parents create a filter that allows them to discern which entertainment options promote a healthy Christian lifestyle.

Section Four

The Spirituality of Millennials

There are young people out there who are willing to make a difference. We should not be labeled as the stereotypical teenager. Everyone is unique.

High school student
Millennial Generation Survey, 2002

Helping Children Find God

Jan R. Knight

Children of any generation have the same spiritual needs: They need to know that there is a God—a God who is always present, a God who loves them with an unconditional love, a God who forgives, a God who creates and loves the creation, a God who can be trusted, a God who is much greater than they can even begin to imagine. They need to belong to families and faith communities that embody these characteristics of God as much as is humanly possible.

What may differ from generation to generation is the context in which children experience these needs. For Millennial-Generation children, this need for God occurs in a context that includes

- an almost overwhelming complexity of world issues;
- more available knowledge, both positive and negative, than the mind can ever hope to assimilate;
- a mobile society that moves family units away from the support of extended family and disrupts ongoing relationships with faith communities;
- demands on time that no longer respect the concept of sabbath time;
- an increasing diversity of population;
- two wage-earner parents or single parents who must of necessity be wage earners, thus decreasing parents' quality time with children and making it more difficult for parents to find time to prepare themselves for and to take seriously their role as spiritual nurturer;
- ever-expanding computer technology, which both offers great benefits and poses potential for great harm from isolation and addiction.

So, how does the church address the spiritual needs of Millennial-Generation children? Above all, the church must consider the spiritual needs of the families of these children, for the primary context for a child's spiritual formation is the family. Even the most active of our children are in the church building two-and-a-half hours on Sunday, perhaps once more during the week, perhaps a little more often during Advent, and perhaps about ten to fifteen hours in vacation Bible school during the summer. This time is critical for a child's faith development, as seeds can be planted and tended. These times of experiencing a wider faith community are essential, but it is in the context of life in the family that the seeds planted in the hours in church grow and bloom—or, for lack of nurture, do not.

For average church-going parents, the responsibility of being spiritual nurturer, if they give much thought to it at all, can seem overwhelming. Many parents simply compartmentalize, so they turn this aspect of their child's development over to the church. Others realize that they have an

Millennial Voices

It's great knowing that God loves you.

Jimmy, elementary-school age

important role in their child's faith development, so they look to their faith community for direction. Often, full of uncertainty about their own faith and harried by the pace of their daily lives, they feel ill-equipped to serve as a spiritual nurturer.

The church has a responsibility not only to the children in its care but also to the parents of those children who need encouragement and support. The church can encourage parents by helping them see that as people who are members of a faith community, as people who are serious about their own faith and who want to grow in their relationship with God, they are indeed equipped to carry out this role of spiritual nurturer in their children's lives. The church can encourage parents by acknowledging that, for parents who are already overloaded, this one more role for them to carry out can seem overwhelming. Then the church can encourage parents by helping them understand that paying attention to God does not have to be added to an already-packed schedule. Rather, it can be woven into the fabric of daily life. The church can encourage parents by helping them know that it is all right that they have not arrived at spiritual maturity themselves, that they may be pretty much where their children are. Parents and children can journey together.

So, how does family life become an arena in which children grow spiritually, with adults growing alongside them? Families need to do and pay attention to many things. Even a cursory reading of those lists, however, shows commonalties that can be stated simply as prayer, storytelling, rituals and traditions, and service to others.

Prayer

Prayer is the foundation. To adapt a familiar adage, the family that prays for and with one another grows in their relationship with God together. For many families, and thus for their children, prayer consists of grace before meals and bedtime prayers. Those prayers are good and appropriate, but what is missing is the sense that prayer is an ongoing conversation with God and that we can pray any time and anywhere. To be able to pray any time and anywhere is, and always has been, an important part of spiritual development. For children of the Millennial Generation, though, this any-time quality of prayer can be a critical understanding—critical because of many of the characteristics of the Millennials' world listed at the beginning of this article. A sense of an ever-present God who loves and accepts them, who wants what is best for them, and who always listens to them can help children through times when they feel alienated because they are in some way different, cut off because of the fast pace and mobility of their society, or confused in the face of too many options, too much information, and too many things.

When adults do not have (and thus cannot model) that sense of God always present, their children are not likely to have that sense as they grow older. Churches can help adults understand that it is never too early (or too late) to begin praying aloud for and with their children. Churches can help parents understand how simple prayers can be incorporated into the natural flow of daily life. They can also help adults understand that they do not have to know the answers to all of

Millennial Voices

I feel safer and closer to God when I am in bed at night. I always pray to him and thank him at night, too.

Erica, elementary-school age

the difficult questions, such as, "Why didn't God answer my prayer?" And they can help children understand that even when they do not understand everything or when they have questions that seem to have no answers, God is still with them, listening for them to pray and caring for them in ways that only God may understand.

Storytelling

Children need to hear faith stories—stories from Scripture, the stories of significant adults in their lives, their own stories, and family and community stories—from a faith perspective. Children have always needed this storytelling, but the Millennial Generation needs it even more. The distractions of our culture—demands that our supercharged lifestyles make on us and places that are literally at our fingertips—make it easy to lose our way. So, telling stories becomes more and more important for each succeeding generation. It is unfortunate when storytelling does not happen frequently in families and in churches, for Scripture stories and personal and family faith stories help children see how faithful people live, understand what it means to be in covenant with God, and see God's hand at work in their lives.

Rituals and Traditions

Like storytelling, family faith rituals and traditions become even more critical for this and succeeding generations as the culture increasingly depersonalizes and uproots. Rituals and traditions help families say, "This is who we are" in the midst of whatever. Traditions link past, present, and future. For Christians, family faith rituals and traditions are a way of saying to the world, "This is what gives our lives meaning. In the midst of whatever culture has to offer, this is where we stand." Rituals and traditions are another way of recognizing God's presence and activity in daily life. Rituals and traditions celebrate transitions in the lives of children and their families and help place all of life in the context of relationship with God.

Service to Others

We often think of growing in relationship with God as an interior thing; but without expression beyond ourselves, our spiritual growth is stunted. The message of the New Testament is one that calls us into service to others. Children generally respond to calls to help others. Children of the Millennial Generation are optimistic and action-oriented; they have a "we are in this together" outlook and value supportive relationships. To fail to respond to these markers of the Millennial Generation from a faith perspective would be to miss an opportunity to help children grow in their relationship with God.

During the writing of this article, the terrible events of September 11, 2001, in New York City and Washington, D.C., have occurred. These events will profoundly affect this Millennial Generation, probably in ways we cannot know at this point. But what we do know about the psyches of children is that when children are given ways to address the difficult issues in the world, they fear less and hope more. When we help

Millennial Voices

On Sundays, my family does things like clean. I haven't been to a church service in four months! Some kids are nice to me in Sunday school, but then at the real school they tease me. It is like they are only nice on Sunday. It really makes me mad!

Allison, elementary-school age

Millennial Voices

I hope something will keep away the bad dreams. Dear Jesus, please send some of your guardian angels to keep away all the bad dreams and thoughts all night. Amen.

Sarah, elementary-school age

- Emphasize using various kinds of prayers with children. For example, with breath prayers one phrase is said as you inhale and a second phrase is said as you exhale. Breath prayers can be said anywhere, any time, until they are as natural as breathing.

- Train adults in what it means to model prayer for children.

- Help adults become more comfortable with various forms of prayer and with praying with children.

- Gather resources for family devotional time.

- Include storytelling time in church family gatherings (Wednesday-night suppers or church picnics).

- Publish a collection of faith stories from families in your church.

- Use All Saints' Day/Halloween as an opportunity for a storytelling festival.

- Compile for parents a list of resources of family rituals and traditions, collect rituals and traditions from the families in your congregation, or create new tradition possibilities.

- Include suggestions for family rituals in the bulletin or newsletter.

- View each family as a whole as a mission and outreach unit.

- Help families with the process of discernment when trying to determine what acts of service they will become involved in.

- Provide opportunities for service for children and for families within the congregation's own outreach ministry.

them understand that our response to those difficult issues comes from heeding Christ's call to us, we help them have faith and hope in something greater than humankind.

Finally, here are some important general needs to remember (again, important for any generation, but growing increasingly important for this and future generations). Millennials need

- to be given room to ask questions and express doubts;
- to have their faith experience accepted, validated for what it is;
- to have a place of love and acceptance, with family as the center;
- to have a faith community that acts as extended family, that nurtures, encourages, and challenges the child and his or her family;
- to have rituals and traditions, markers that help the child know who and whose she or he is.

Discerning God's Will

Julie O'Neal

As a young adult, Julie was faced with a critical decision. This article invites you to share in her journey of discovery and discernment.

At one time or another, we all have had to make decisions in our lives. Whether it is as simple as choosing what to eat for breakfast or more involved like deciding what to buy a friend for a birthday, we use processes to help us make the best decisions.

When we are faced with tough choices and big decisions, a ready decision-making process becomes an important part of the outcome. Who we turn to and our method of discernment or understanding can help us make an informed, beneficial, and appropriate decision.

Not long ago, I made the decision to enter seminary. That decision was a major step in my life. In order to make the decision, I used a process that helped me make that choice.

Since I grew up in the church where my father was a pastor, being in church quickly became an important part of my life. As I approached young adulthood, being in church was no longer something that I had to do but something that I wanted to do. In college, I majored in religious studies, and I felt that God wanted me to work in the church. Although I thought that being a pastor was not where I was to be, I was unsure of what I was to do. Graduation was approaching rapidly, and I was still trying to figure out what to do with my life, where I was headed. I was pressured about the decisions that lay ahead. Through my involvement with the church, though, I was able to attend a meeting with people from all of the thirteen United Methodist seminaries. In conversation with several people there, I began to explore what seminaries are all about.

At this point in my decision-making process, I was doing detail work. I began to look at the details of all the seminaries: where each one was located in the United States, what sort of degree programs would be interesting to me, what options in ministry outside the typical considerations I might explore. In a sense, I was investigating whether or not attending seminary would be a possibility for me. I was also trying to look for ways that attending seminary may not be right for me. In the process, I considered what I was good at and what patterns of my activities would best suit a certain degree. I began conversations with others whom I trusted to help me make an informed decision. I knew that God had plans for me, but were these plans I was making God's plans? Thus began the discernment process.

I began to spend much time in prayer with God about this decision—asking questions, requesting a sign, listening to God, and trying

Talking with other people and being around others who are also going through some hard times is good and healthy.

- Affirm the person who is struggling with a tough decision, reminding him or her that struggling is a healthy process. That person is not alone.

- Offer times of support, whether it is praying with the person who is struggling or helping him or her reflect on God's actions in his or her life.

- Plan regular meeting times when he or she can express feelings and thoughts.

- Provide resources that will help him or her make an informed decision.

to understand what God was telling me. I knew that it was important to keep my ears, eyes, and heart open to what God was calling me to do. I wanted to feel confident and not detached from any decision I made about attending seminary.

Eventually, I decided I would refocus myself. One way I did this was to keep a prayer journal. I wrote my thoughts, my fears, my questions, my ideas, and my concerns in the journal. I searched the Scriptures for answers to the waves of questions that kept coming. Some answers came easily; others were not as clear.

Friends and family were essential in my decision-making process. They provided listening ears to my concerns and my excitements. They were an objective voice when I could not see other sides of an issue. They reminded me of their love and support, which would be there whatever I decided. Knowing that their support was there was comforting when I considered leaving everything that was familiar. My family and friends were there when I visited the schools I was considering, helping me feel comfortable and get a sense of what the experience was really like. They were there when I was doing more detail work and seeking answers to logistical questions. It was a blessing to know that people were there during my questioning, searching, and struggling. I began to look for signs that God was in this decision that I was beginning to make. I recognized God manifested in the dew on the grass. It was sort of like God saying to me, "A new time has come. Prepare, for there is a change coming." After much prayer, I finally decided to attend seminary. It was good to finally celebrate in this new beginning that was to commence.

God continued to be with me during the days of preparing, leaving the familiar, and arriving at a new place. Flowing through people who were close to me, God's grace and assurance helped me face the days of uncertainty, loneliness, doubts, and fear. Yet, after I began to settle in, the questioning began to creep in again. I felt the need for extra time to process some of the things that I had been feeling. I began to second-guess myself and wondered if I had made a mistake. My thoughts and feelings became a battle of mixed emotions. I knew that I should be open and discover the gifts, talents, and ways that I am to be used, while in the meantime feeling homesick, lonely, scared, intimidated, and needing love, reassurance, and a hug.

At the height of my fear and uncertainty, I decided to watch the sunset, hoping that it would bring me some much-needed peace and inner strength. I felt God's presence in the sunset, in the many colors and layers in the sky. It was ironic, the beautiful sunset on the outside contrasting with the inner turmoil that I was feeling on the inside.

I knew that God loves me for who I am, but I also knew that God loves me for who I am to become. Only God knows who that is. The questions came: Did I have enough trust to depend on God wholly? Did God trust in me so much that even through all of these emotions, I would be able to know that I was doing the right thing? Yet, I would wait for God's direction.

It was not an easy time, and the answers did not come quickly. But I was patient, trusting in God, listening to God, searching for ways that God's grace and peace affirmed my decision. The affirmations did not always come in forms that I expected; but slowly, and by looking closely, they did appear. By asking to be filled with God's amazing presence and to be made aware of God's deeds, I was able to become a vessel of God's love, helping me see the way that God wants me to be. God worked, and continues to work, in me and through me to minister to others. Through that giving of myself, I began to receive divine blessings in return. I have begun to accept my unknowing and uncertainty, finding God in the midst of it all, confident in the fact that although I do not know, God does.

With this God-inspired confidence, I am aware that I still do not know all the answers—and I may never have them revealed. But I can learn and grow, hopeful for the things yet to come. I am content that things do not have to be planned out to the last detail for God's plan to work out.

A few weeks ago, I went out again to watch the sunset. It was with new friends, during a new year, and with a new perspective. By combining constant time in prayer and in God-based reflection with friends and family who offered me a listening ear and honest and objective discussions, I was able to make one of the most important decisions in my life.

Making Decisions

Engaging in certain practices will help you discern God's will in any decisions that you might make. These practices may include, but are not limited to,

- spending time in prayer, talking with God, listening to God, looking for ways that God is active and present in your decision;
- engaging in honest conversations with people you trust, people who can help you make wise decisions;
- recording in a journal your thoughts, ideas, questions and ways your questions have been answered, along with passages of Scripture or words of wisdom that are significant.

Millennial Voices

My faith in the Lord is who I am; it has made me the person I am today, and the person I will become in the future.

Lisa, age 17

What Your Church Can Do

- Offer workshops or small-group sessions to focus on God's will and decision making.

- Pair up groups—singles with junior high youth, young adults with older adults, and so forth—to be mentors to one another.

- Offer prayer times for those who are going through big decisions.

Guide for Discernment

Identify the decision to be made:

Set up times for in-depth prayer:

Identify people who can help you reflect on your choices:

Make appointments to meet with the people listed above:

Record thoughts, ideas, and questions related to the decision to be made:

The Power of Turning Points

Kevin Witt

Talk about God and Christ leaves most Millennials uninspired. They breathe and move in an information environment. They can access libraries of religious concepts with the click of a mouse. Many see little need for the church simply as a purveyor of religious ideas. Fortunately, a pervasive longing to actually experience God opens the door for church communities and for people who embody their faith. Call it skepticism or astute wisdom; but if words fail to live in day-to-day joys and struggles, then this Millennial Generation knows how to make choices and to opt out. They seek a direct experience of Christian love and faith, not a description.

Identify Turning Points

As Christian spiritual leaders, how can we cooperate with the Holy Spirit to encourage young people to sense the presence of God in the midst of real-life situations? We can look for the transition zones, or the turning points, in the lives of the young people themselves. Change or the prospect of change opens up new possibilities like nothing else. The furrow between the familiar and the frontier of new experience is incredibly fertile. Seeds planted there have great opportunity to take root and grow deep in God. The Millennial Generation's thirst for experience over indoctrination, along with the sheer volume of new opportunities and happenings inherent during the high school and young-adult years, makes it especially important to appreciate the potential of transitions of all kinds as prime occasions for spiritual growth.

The potency of transitions has long been observed by a wide variety of disciplines. Biology teaches us about transition zones, the places where two ecosystems come together. At the juncture between land and water or between field and forest, a greater variety of life exists. In similar fashion, a proliferation of possibilities occurs for a human being whenever he or she crosses over from one situation to another. Among those possibilities is knowing and experiencing God in new ways.

Psychology reveals that change frequently elicits heightened awareness and feeling. The unfamiliar can produce fear, sorrow, joy, inspiration, or many other intensely felt expressions. What taps into our emotions at this level quite often becomes imprinted in our memory. What we remember continues to shape us for a lifetime. Imagine the impact of attaching the love of Christ to these memories through actions and conversations that build relationships of trust with young people. These caring friendships free them to share even more of the twists and turns that really matter to them.

Millennial Voices

I changed schools a few times. There were moments when I felt really left out, like I didn't belong. Once I went through that experience, it changed me. I treat people differently now because I know their pain. I think that's God with me—working in my life to teach me. I am more outgoing to help others feel included and wanted.

Briana, age 16

Educators know the effectiveness of experiential learning. Learning that engages the full spectrum of mind, body, and spirit has the greatest chance of becoming a way of life. Learning that offers direct application to actual experiences in other areas of life motivates retention and incorporation. It is for this reason that the most influential teachers not only know what concepts they want to pass on but also seek to know their students. Mentors strive to understand what their students care about—their opportunities, their interests, their perspectives, their circumstances, their celebrations, and their struggles—so that intentional faith connections can be made.

Glimpse the Sacred

It is crucial to grasp that just knowing about the passages in the lives of young people, in and of itself, does not suffice. An essential catalyst must be added to the mix in order for them to catch a glimpse of the sacred. That catalyst involves reflecting on the situation with God in mind, becoming aware of God's loving presence in the ordinary and not so ordinary. This awareness is the work of the Holy Spirit made visible through those of us who are spiritual friends. It is not only what we say but also what we do that inspires fresh awareness. What is commonly viewed as curriculum or program pales in comparison to building significant relationships and sharing real-life experience. It may seem trite, but simply inviting others to seek God in their own situations often makes all the difference.

Even though the Bible was not written specifically to address the points being made here, it abounds with examples. Much of the Bible is actual accounts of people's journeys and their own recognition of God. Joseph's life takes an unexpected turn when his brothers betray him and when he comes to know the faithfulness of the Lord in a place far from home (Genesis 37 and 39–45). Esther faces a huge dilemma when new laws are enacted that threaten the well-being of her people. She must choose whether or not to risk her own position, and much more, to have these laws repealed. Through the urging of a spiritual mentor, Mordecai, she is able to reflect on her life and realize that God has given her the opportunity to be a person of influence "for just such a time as this" (Esther 4). Jesus encounters a woman in the mundane routine of drawing water from a well. This unplanned meeting and conversation intrigues her because a Jewish rabbi actually speaks with her, knowing full well she is a woman and a Samaritan. In listening and talking, Jesus alters the way she understands thirst and water forever. She sees God with new eyes. Every trip to draw water for the rest of her life may remind her to ponder the God of living water (John 4:4-30).

Create Shared Experiences

In addition to tapping the unplanned teachable moments that arise in the lives of people themselves, Jesus creates shared experiences. After dinner, Jesus takes a simple towel and basin and washes his friends' feet. He asks them, "Do you know what I have done to you?" In that time of teacher serving student, the active experience of who

God is, they begin to grasp the nature of God's love and learn what it means to be Spirit-led leaders (John 13:3-17).

The Millennial Generation longs for a community of faith that values them enough to actually befriend them and walk by their side through the turning points of their own existence. They are looking for experiences of Emmanuel, God is with us. Some meaningful interactions await us if we move out among the people of this generation. An incredible search is underway where young people live their daily lives. We may not feel completely capable in our ability as spiritual guides, friends, relatives, and mentors; however, we do not undertake this task alone. Jesus assures us that God's Spirit is present and involved when people sincerely seek God. Be heartened, for our task is not to provide all the answers or to somehow conjure up God for others. Our role as people who care and serve the children, youth, and young adults in our families, neighborhoods, and community is simply to encourage them to ask, to search, and to knock. A divine promise is given to every new generation.

"Ask, and it will be given you; search, and you will find; knock, and the door will be opened for you. For everyone who asks receives, and everyone who searches finds, and for everyone who knocks, the door will be opened" (Matthew 7:7-8).

Some Pointers

1. Get out where the young people are. Be with them and learn what is important to them.
2. Recruit parents and other adults to establish spiritual friendships with young people. Help them learn how to be aware of the changes young people are going through. Offer support.
3. Most adults can establish relationships at this level with only two to five young people at any one time. Get more adults involved or establish small groups designed as time for young people to talk deeply about their lives together and to connect with God.
4. Train parents and mentors about how to have spiritual conversations and how to help young people notice God's presence in everyday situations.
5. Read books to learn more about ministry with young people today. The following are a good start: *Twists of Faith: Ministry With Youth at the Turning Points of Their Lives,* by Marcey Balcomb and Kevin Witt (Discipleship Resources, 1999), and *The Godbearing Life: The Art of Soul-Tending for Youth Ministry,* by Kenda Creasy Dean and Ron Foster (Upper Room, 1998).

What Your Church Can Do

Family still has the greatest influence on young people, so launch faith formation within families and at home.

- Teach families how to enhance relationships of mutual respect and care with the young people in their midst.

- Encourage adults to listen supportively to young people talk about what is happening and what is important in their lives.

- Teach parents and adult role models how to have conversations and to create experiences that encourage young people to think about God and how Christ's way of love connects with real life.

- Provide resources for families that help them incorporate spiritual practices—such as journaling, family prayer, Bible reflection, rites of passage, and so forth—that give young people a chance to connect with God and to reflect on their experiences with God in mind.

- Remind adult family members to live a life of faith with integrity through the twists and turns they face, for these examples truly motivate young people to seek God, too.

The Littleton Effect

John Gooch

Fifteen people died violently at Columbine High School in Littleton, Colorado, on April 20, 1999. It was the latest in a series of horrible incidents: Pearl, Mississippi; West Paducah, Kentucky; Jonesboro, Arkansas; Fayetteville, Tennessee; Springfield, Oregon. After Columbine there were incidents at Fort Gibson, Oklahoma, and at Wedgwood Baptist Church, Fort Worth, Texas. The nation was rightly horrified and alarmed. But look at some facts. In 1992–93, there were fifty-five violent deaths in schools. In 1998–99, there were twenty-five, including Columbine. More than twenty million teens attend U.S. high schools every day, so these youth are far more likely to be killed by lightning than by a school shooting.[1]

This harsh statement of reality is not to downplay the emotional power of school violence. Youth have developed a dread of mass gun killings, just because they are so spectacular. Columbine, in particular, has captured teenagers' attention. The initial response to Columbine, and related incidents, was the spontaneous development of a theology of martyrdom among youth. At Columbine High School, Cassie Bernall was shot just after she said she believed in God. At Wedgwood Baptist Church, youth were shielding one another with their bodies while the shots were being fired. In each case, there was a close connection between faith and death.

So, perhaps the primary element of the Littleton Effect is that youth are becoming aware that they could die. They are beginning to see a special connection to God as something people their own age are willing to die for. Before they die, today's youth want their lives to mean something; they do not want to live or die for nothing. This awareness of death and meaning leads to basic questions about salvation: What is worth dying for? What is worth living for? Does anyone care enough about me to die for me?

Two members of Cassie Bernall's youth group were in the same room with her when she was shot. They escaped unharmed, and one way they make sense of all the horror of that day is to tell the story of their friend who died because she believed in God. They saw her as willing to die for her love of God. Now, true love is always worth dying for, as any *Titanic* fan can tell you. But the matter goes deeper than that. Youth sense that their salvation lies in finding love. What do I love enough to live for? What do I love enough to die for? Who loves me enough to die for me? Those are some of the key questions raised for youth—and in some ways for all of us—as a part of the Littleton Effect.

These are questions about salvation that have roots deep in the Christian experience. Jesus said to his disciples, "No one has greater love than this, to lay down one's life for one's friends" (John 15:13).

If the key questions raised by the Littleton Effect are questions about salvation, what does that mean for how we minister to the Millennial Generation? One possibility is that the kinds of entertainment ministries we have used in the past to try to involve more youth in church activities will not cut it anymore. In fact, we might attract more youth by helping them ask their questions about salvation and meaning—and by helping them struggle to find some answers. It may well be that the most successful ministries to Millennial youth will involve seeking salvation, rather than organizing trips to water parks and ski slopes.

Youth Identity and God Questions

Who am I? Who is God? Who is my neighbor? These three questions are closely related. How we see ourselves affects how we see God and our neighbors. How we see God affects how we see ourselves and others. For example, a youth who sees God as a sort of celestial Santa Claus, always making lists of when we have been good and when we have been bad, will have a hard time finding a good self-image. It is hard to feel good about yourself if all your spiritual energy goes into trying to be good enough to please God, and knowing you cannot make it. But if that same youth becomes aware that God's nature is love and that God cares more about forgiveness than about keeping lists, her or his self-image will change. The new self-image will be more positive and free. Relationships with neighbors will also change as love and acceptance become a part of all relationships. Another example: youth who believe that unconditional love is a new law they have to live up to in order to please God have a hard time feeling good about themselves because they cannot live up to what they think God wants. On the other hand, youth who come back from a serious mission trip wanting to do more to serve others will have more positive images of both God and themselves.

The search for self is also a search for God. Saint Augustine, a great Christian thinker (354–430), once said that God has made us for Godself and that our hearts will always be restless until they find rest in God. The quest for identity and the quest for God go hand in hand. Youth are trying to discover who they are. Their quest means, among other things, that they have to choose every day between relationships that affirm them and help them grow and isolation that leads to self-destruction. The most basic, affirming relationship is the relationship with God. This reality alone makes salvation a central, even if unspoken, theme in adolescence

For youth, salvation always comes in relationships. Relationships create the kind of intimacy that affirms existence. Youth long for love and faithfulness—and the ultimate source for satisfying that longing is God. When youth follow their longing into a relationship with God, they discover that they are loved, are made new and whole, and find joy and meaning for their lives. Suddenly there is something (a relationship with God) worth dying for. And, if it is worth dying for, it is surely worth living for. One effect of Littleton has been to bring those issues into sharper focus.

What Is Most Important in Life?

This question about importance in life is a key question. If youth are not in touch with what is important, they may feel that life has no meaning. A sense of meaninglessness can lead to depression or even to self-destructive behaviors, such as drinking, smoking, sexual promiscuity, and so forth. Or, depression might lead to violence toward others.

So, what is important? That question is closely related to three other questions youth must answer: Who am I? What does my life mean? What am I going to do with my life? These are crucial questions that youth, of any generation, have to answer as they mature. It may be that identifying values is another key element in youth ministry to Millennials (who are the only youth we have with whom to minister): What is most important in life? What does my life mean? Who am I, and what is important about my life? These questions go hand in hand with the question, What is worth dying for?

The place to begin in finding the answers to all these questions is God and the wonder of God's love. The Christian faith is often presented as a call to self-sacrifice, just as Jesus gave up his life on the cross. Certainly, the spontaneous appearance of a theology of martyrdom among youth after Columbine would reinforce this idea of sacrifice. But there is a counter theme in Christian faith to which we also need to pay attention. Why did God think the cross was so necessary? Why does God care about us enough that Jesus died to express that caring? Certainly it is not because God needs to sacrifice; nor is it because God feels an obligation to save us. So, why does God care about us? Because Love always delights in the beloved. The Song of Songs (The Song of Solomon, a sometimes obscure book in the Bible) reminds us of the power of human love. Our tradition has taught us that the power of human love is like a faint image of God's love for us. Love is a theme with which adolescents can identify. They can get into the Song of Songs on a human level. As they develop relationships with other people, or even fall in love, they are willing and eager to make sacrifices for the one they love. Nothing is too good for their special friend, or for their sweetheart. Out of that experience of love, they are ready to hear about the Song of Songs as an expression of God's passionate longing for us. God takes delight in who we are and what our lives are about. And it is out of that delight and love that God makes sacrifices for us. The cross is real. But what makes it real is God's delight in us and desire for us.

So, What Is the Littleton Effect?

In the long run, the Littleton Effect is not simply increased security in schools or a new emphasis on gun control. It is not even fear of mass violence. In the long run, the Littleton Effect is the awareness of a deep longing on the part of youth for salvation—for the awareness of a love (a relationship with God) that is worth dying for and, therefore, worth living for. This Littleton Effect is a significant key to youth ministry with the Millennials in our churches.

Endnote

1 *Millennials Rising: The Next Great Generation,* by Neil Howe and William Strauss (New York: Vintage Books/Random House, 2000), page 209.

Pointers for Pastors

Preach a series of sermons on salvation. As a part of your preparation, meet with the youth in your congregation and ask about what they most need, how they feel about God caring for them, and about their various images of salvation.

What Your Church Can Do

Rethink the curriculum for your ministry with youth. Are you actually dealing with the substantive questions youth are asking? Use youth as consultants in the process.

Millennials and
Community Service

Bill Crenshaw

Prior to September 11, 2001, social scientists had all but concluded that the Columbine High School tragedy would stand as the defining moment for the Millennial Generation. The attack on the World Trade Center in New York City, however, makes the Columbine incident look minuscule by comparison. The kids who have grown up with peace and prosperity are now facing what may be the defining moment for their generation: September 11, or the 9/11 attack. The question has been asked repeatedly, "How will young people cope?"

While many young people were still reeling in shock, horror, and dismay after the events of September 11, 2001, others were moving beyond the shock to action. Blood donation centers were flooded with thousands of young college students and young working adults. They continually echoed the need to do something. Even the youngest of students in America, elementary- to high school-aged kids, engaged in such fundraising activities as lemonade stands, walk-a-thons, and car washes all across the nation. Proceeds from their efforts were sent to the Red Cross and to funds for victims of the World Trade Center tragedy. College students took advantage of network air time to vent feelings and responses to the tragedy. Young campus leaders were among the first to speak of the shifting reality from secure, carefree lifestyles to a new reality of fear and uncertainty spurred by terrorist violence.

Demographers characterize Millennials as the most protected, encouraged, and anticipated generation of children in the nation's history. Protected to overprotected may be a fair assessment, considering increasing advocacy for children's rights, which extends as far as a child divorcing his or her parents, numerous screening processes for workers with children and youth, and intentional measures to protect children and communities from convicted child molesters. A sharp rise in the number of children being home schooled should be added to the mix.

Despite efforts to protect this generation from harm and danger, major instances of violence and destruction have yet prevailed. The bombing of the Murrah Federal Building in Oklahoma City and repeated instances of gun violence in schools at all levels were significant emotional events. Ironically, some of the most notable violence was committed by teenagers in the Columbine, southern Mississippi, and Kentucky school shootings. This generation has also grown up during a time in which domestic and family violence is common. These instances and situations breed fear, anxiety, and uncertainty.

This generation has also grown up in the midst of numerous positive messages. Consumer advertising is full of preadolescents and teens as individuals in control of situations and as subject-matter experts. These commercials fill prime-time TV programming slots. The intrinsic messages of "you have value," "you have power," and "you can control" anchor deeply in the minds of the young. Consumer research consistently names the ten- to thirteen-year-old crowd as being perhaps the most savvy of shoppers. They are known for making informed buying decisions. Confidence to decide and act is reflected in children, adolescents, and younger adults. Measurable fear and seeming confidence may account for paradoxical effects with this generation.

This is also the first generation of Americans to grow up in an era of service learning. Community service was emphasized with Postmoderns and others. Today, middle schools and high schools have students engaged in community work or service as part of the curriculum. This emphasis of service learning parallels an emphasis given to fitness and physical education in public schools during the Kennedy-Johnson era of the sixties. Involvement in civic organizations and service learning organizations, such as the Boy Scouts and Girl Scouts of America and Boys/Girls Clubs of America, is dramatically up, which confirms that a new service ethic is emerging.

The community service ethic of Millennials differs, however, from the spirit of being in service to America that began during the Kennedy-Johnson era and continued through the seventies. This group seems prone to collegial action, are supportive of civic institutions, and strive for immediate, tangible results. This is in sharp contrast to the social movement of the late sixties and seventies, where individuals who were anti-establishment and anti-institution sought to make changes with long-term effects. It is interesting to watch Millennials band together quickly in groups and take action.

At the huge United Methodist Youth gathering of more than 9,000, also known as Youth '99, a call for volunteers to work 40 telephone prayer lines was given during a morning plenary. More than 250 youth showed up at the prayer center ready to work the phones. After the 40 volunteers were selected to work the telephone stations, the remaining young people chose, on their own accord, to stay at the prayer center, form prayer circles, and pray for the telephone workers and situations facing youth all over the world. As a group, energized Millennials rarely walk away from an opportunity to get something meaningful done.

The countless lemonade stands and car washes that followed in the wake of the attack on the World Trade Center reflect this observation. These efforts, however small, were opportunities to connect and make contributions to the huge relief efforts across the nation. Their broad perspective was further reflected in the post-9/11 college campus activities where students packed teach-ins and classes on international relations, the Middle East, and Islamic and Arabic studies. Students were anxious to quickly gather information that helped them understand the complexities of the World Trade Center attack and global activities in its aftermath. Millennials seem less inclined to assume or blame and more intent to search for understanding. Students have also flocked to teach-ins on hate crimes and racial-cultural profiling.

What seems clear, in the wake of the 9/11 tragedy, is a growing shift from widespread apathy with politics and campus activism of the 1990's to central issues that are igniting action. Millennials are the most informed generation of young people and young adults so far. They have studied Western, African, and Asian history and cultures. Many have ventured beyond their own cultures to date, live with, and experience other cultures and religions. They represent the most diverse population within adult segments. They really champion a spirit of tolerance.

National Public Radio recently spoke with a small group of students from Haverford College, a small liberal arts college in Pennsylvania, about the war on terrorism. The circle of students spoke openly and passionately about their feelings and beliefs about United States foreign policy and Afghanistan. One sophomore student posed an interesting alternative to warfare as the means to resolve our nation's tragedy: What if a collective force of 200,000 Westerners went to Afghanistan to pursue a dialogue with the Afghan people? He was convinced that Americans have as much need to be understood as they need to understand Afghan and Islamic people across the world. He further underscored this seemingly strange idea by suggesting that dialogue leads to understanding, and that understanding enhances assistance and cooperation. Hmm…

Questions for Reflection and Action

- Considering that Millennials act in groups or clusters, willingly align with institutions perceived as purposeful, strive to accomplish measurable results with their actions, and champion a spirit of inclusion, how might the church help young people in this generation further act responsibly to events, situations, and conditions of the world? How might leaders encourage and facilitate deeper post-experience reflections?

- While service learning courses and activities are prevalent in public schools and on college campuses, educators and researchers have questioned whether these courses and experiences are impacting students on a deeper level. Students are sensitive to the urgent needs of others, but they are seldom challenged to act on the greater systems that continue to create inequities in the lives of many. Activists point to a lack of critical thinking with service action. How might your congregation, faith community or group, or faith community leaders partner or enter into an alliance with a local campus ministry to foster greater consciousness for social action with such engagements?

- In the post-9/11 era, college students and working young adults are clearly rethinking choices at critical junctures in their lives. The idea of working with the government, working in the medical field, even entering the military is growing in popularity. How might adults in your congregation enter into mentoring relationships with Millennials who are entering the workforce and striking out on their own?

- Fear, whether founded or unfounded, still binds the lives of many young people. What actions can parents and caregivers take as loving, supportive adults to guide young people to healing and wholeness?

What Is Success?

Terry B. Carty

In the past, success in youth ministries has often been defined by the numbers of participants. Unfortunately, the church's preoccupation with declining membership has sometimes spawned youth ministries that are more focused on keeping youth coming than on faith formation. When asked to introduce themselves, youth workers will name, without prompting, their church and tell the size of their youth group. When asked what they have accomplished, though, they often have to think a while to offer answers beyond numbers.

Leaders of children's ministries often count success by pointing to newly renovated, child-friendly space, a state-of-the-art playground, or new children's choir robes. They enjoy citing numbers of children in Sunday school and vacation Bible school. They can tell you how many they have in Parent's Day Out or in the afterschool program. Yet, they often operate for weeks at a time without reflecting on their carefully worded mission statements.

Young-adult ministries usually do not have the problem of being too focused on the numbers game; they usually have nothing to brag about. The church has failed dismally to be in ministry with eighteen- to thirty-year-olds. In young-adult ministry, it is counted as success to simply have one.

If We Get Where We Are Going, Where Will We Be?

Craig Miller's introduction to the Millennial Generation in this book describes a generation of young people who face a lot of pressure to succeed. They are conditioned by educational methods that prepare them to survive in a competitive world. Often, it is more important for them to be among the top scorers in the class than to learn the content of the lessons. Millennials are encouraged to compare their work with that of others, rather than comparing it with an internal standard of excellence; that is, a value system. Families have subscribed to the cultural value of being normal, so maintenance of the right external appearance and the work of trying to fit in dominate family life and its finances.

The church in North America does little to challenge the effects of today's culture. Sermons often lead people to believe that God endorses their lifestyles. Sunday school lessons assure children and youth that "Jesus loves you," but they are often soft on "take up your cross and follow." The church does well in a culture of fitting in, but the church falls considerably short of its mission of pressing for a distinctively countercultural discipleship lifestyle.

DemoFacts

Where do you plan to go after high school?

91%	College
4%	Military
3%	Full-Time Work
2%	Trade School

Millennial Generation Survey, 2002

If we get where we are going, we may well be standing in a pool of mediocrity. *Mediocre* is a word from Latin roots that literally means halfway up the mountain. Mediocre is not good, but it is also not bad. But, like a mountain climber, you may be stuck halfway between your goal and not having tried at all.

What Is a Successful Person?

It is important for the church to use its resources to redefine what it means to be successful. What is success? Success is realizing the gifts and talents that God has given, developing those gifts, and using them in supporting the human family. Success is seeking and fulfilling one's call, or vocation. Vocation may lead to a lucrative career. Or it may not. Some may need to work in a job that is not directly related to his or her call in order to make a living. A vocation, then, may lead to volunteer work, a different way of focusing on one's job, or seeking the right job. Success, then, is fulfilling the will of God, and success will be recognized by the joy such fulfillment brings.

Young people today are seeking success. They are watching adults for models of what culture identifies as successful and are setting strategies to become like those adults. These strategies often lead to careers that pay a lot of money but are unfulfilling, may lead to tangible success by illegal or immoral means, and can lead to a lot of unhappiness in life.

What Is a Successful Ministry?

A successful ministry with young people is one that defines success in terms that are consistent with the kingdom of God. Successful ministry is measured by its impact on the spiritual growth of people. It is one that helps young people recognize their success by the joy they experience when they are acting according to the will of God. A successful ministry is measured by changed lives, transformed to being more Christlike. A successful ministry considers people as they are, enables them to discover God's will for their lives, and helps them develop their gifts toward that end.

Applying What We Know

Throughout its history, the church has used Scripture and tradition to guide young people through processes of becoming mature adults. No matter what has been the course of world events, the church has offered direction. Now it is time to apply the knowledge we have about characteristics of the Millennial Generation and the emerging trends in their culture (see the Introduction on pages 13–26) to ways we can help young people today find success that brings joy. God's word in Scripture and traditional Christian practices still join with human reason and experience to provide the necessary tools to meet the needs of this generation.

Strong Families

Our Israelite and Christian heritage models a high value on the family from generation to generation. In addition to providing human nurturing, the family has always been the primary faith-forming center in that tradition. The church of today must not see itself outside of the family but must be central to the family. Families today find themselves torn apart and rebuilt and shaped in many different ways. Scripture and history tell us that this is not unusual. When families have been separated by famine, captivity, war, and internal strife, those remaining have pulled together to share in the parenting of the young. The church must use its resources to help them join with one another to raise their young people.

Healthy Relationships

Young people need to form positive identities and to feel good about themselves. The church must help them find ways to be in relationships that build up rather than diminish. These relationships, which model those of Christ, must use the power of confession and forgiveness and must be built on the conviction that God has created each individual for a good purpose in God's kingdom. The Gospels give us a glimpse of the relationships that Christ had with disciples, followers, and strangers. This glimpse is enough to form a foundation for teaching and living in healthy relationships.

Security

Security has become a primary concern for the Millennial Generation. Terrorism and school violence have created an environment of fear that seeks sanctuary. The church has always been seen as a place of safety. The church's teaching about God's creation and protection of the world can minimize the anxiety and chaos that surrounds young people. A stable and predictable environment in worship and religious education helps young people know the safety of God's people.

Discernment Tools and Skills

Young people are exposed to varying concepts of success, so the church must teach tools and skills for spiritual discernment. With the coming of the modern age, many of these practices are viewed as ineffective because they are not scientific. Yet, when exercised, the practices related to spiritual discernment continue to be the most effective in helping young people find God's direction for their lives. If the church can prepare the Millennials for spiritual discernment, it is more likely that the youth boom will focus on service rather than on possessions. Discernment will help young people focus on God's people rather than only on themselves.

Coping Skills

Although fear of violence and an unsure economy are new to many Americans, others have lived in that environment all their lives. The Christian faith is built on a theology of hope for oppressed people. For those who feel powerless, Christianity provides skills for abundant living in spite of forces that seem overwhelming. The church can help young people discover their boundaries and encourage realistic expectations for living based on Christian rather than secular values. For the Millennial Generation, this Christian living will require that leaders listen to the voices of young people in order to help them identify real, rather than perceived, boundaries.

Exposure to Different Cultures

It is inevitable that young people will be exposed to cultures other than their own. The images they receive from the media (especially on TV and in the movies) can sometimes cause fear or distrust. With this kind of indirect exposure to cultures, young people are susceptible to stereotypes and fear of others based on racial profiling. They are curious about the differences; and if they remain uninformed, they will imagine greater differences than really exist. In communities where cultural and ethnic diversity already exist, it is important to answer the questions youth have about their experiences. In situations where direct exposure outside of one's own cultural/ethnic background are delayed until one goes somewhere else (college or work), it is even more important for the church to have taught about acceptance and tolerance. This teaching can be supplemented by church-sponsored travel for service and/or learning in different cultural settings.

Asset Development

Social competencies are critical to the success of an individual in any society. The church must pay attention to this reality even in light of its efforts to be countercultural. It is important to develop assets in young people that are consistent with the church's commitment. The church can help develop many assets, not the least of which are commitment to lifelong learning, peaceful conflict-resolution skills, tolerance and acceptance of other worldviews, and knowledge and use of the practices of Christian faith.

Leader Development

The Millennial Generation seems to be a new civic generation, with characteristics similar to those of the GIs. Since they are the ones who will be leading our world into its next era, it is important that they be raised as strong spiritual leaders. The church must teach the Christian faith by both lesson and example. Current church leaders must be intentional about using decision-making processes that seek the will of God. Church programs must reflect Christian theology in both their content and teaching methods. Young men and women must be given equal access to learning to be leaders and to opportunities to practice their skills in the church.

Access to Technology

For Millennials, one aspect of poverty is the inability to access the latest technology. While the majority of Millennials have access to computers and the Internet, many do not have ways to be part of the information revolution. For centuries, the church has sought to overcome powerlessness and poverty by providing education. Today, the church can address the lack of access by providing computer labs, by training young people in the use of the latest technology, or by helping young people obtain access through public libraries or other sources.

Advocacy

Advocacy for young people means standing for their empowerment to be heard in places where youth have traditionally had no voice. It means lobbying for acceptance of the opinions of young people. Jesus modeled a ministry of empowerment by removing things that block people from responding to God's call. This model included healing people so that their disease did not set them apart from society, empowering women as spiritual leaders, and giving children direct access to his teaching and care. It is the work of the church, the body of Christ, to remove impediments that young people face in responding to God in their lives.

Spirituality

With the focus of so many young people on spirituality, the church has a unique responsibility to provide spiritual guidance for those who are searching for spiritual truth. Young people need both information about and experiences of the living God. The church is rather new to the information age and its technology, but it has centuries of experience in proven practices that have consistently connected people to God. If the church does not help young people with their spiritual yearnings, we can only imagine who will.

Pressing on Toward the Goal

The young people of the Millennial Generation are seeking meaning and purpose in their lives. They are looking at images in magazines, on televisions, and on computer monitors. They are consulting with friends to gather information that will make them successful. The church's success in ministries with young people is inseparably connected to the quest of young people for success.

The church is being called to live its life and do its ministry in such a way that young people see it as a primary resource in their search for meaning. The people of the church are being called to faithfulness in their discipleship to Jesus Christ. It is in living the Christian life that we earn the respect of others whom we hope to influence by our uniqueness. It is time for Christians to remember who we are and whose we are. In remembering Christ, the disciples, the martyrs, and all the saints who have gone before us, we find the examples that will lead young people to an understanding of true success.

What Your Church Can Do

Meet with principals and other community leaders to ask the following:

- What are the needs of the children and youth in your community?
- What pressures are families feeling?
- How are the various options that children and youth have helping or harming them?
- How is the community helping those who are being left behind?

Section Five

Models for Ministry With Millennials

We enter the world of the Millennial Generation not only to offer them Jesus but also to learn from the Jesus in them.

"The Pastor's Role With Millennials," by Rob Weber,
in *Making God Real for a New Generation;* page 151.

Creating a Discipleship System for Youth and Young Adults

Terry B. Carty and Susan H. Hay

Jimmy is a wonderful swimming teacher. Starting with children as young as age three and with classes no larger than ten learners, Jimmy patiently moves children from tentatively stepping into the pool, to playing in the shallow end, to moving to the deeper end, and finally to jumping off a low diving board. Each year on the first day of swimming lessons, the children come with their parents to hear together what they will be doing, what supplies they will need to bring each time they come, what the expectations are for attendance, how discipline will be handled, and what the parents should be doing while their children are learning how to swim. Jimmy has a system, a mission and vision for teaching. He knows what business he is in, and he aligns all of his activities toward achieving his mission.

Jimmy's process of teaching has within it images of the Christian's journey in faith and discipleship: being invited, stepping in, wading, going deeper, and immersing (jumping off the diving board). When people become consciously aware of their connection with God, a desire develops within them to know more about God. Sometimes the desire is subtle, hardly noticeable; at other times, it is powerful and life changing. As leaders of youth and young adults, we ask, "What can I do to assist people on their faith and discipleship journeys into going deeper? How do I create a discipleship system for youth and young adults that is sustainable?"

Our Biblical Foundation

Two Scriptures ground us in making disciples. In 1 Corinthians 12:12-26, Paul proclaims that we are all part of one body. When one member of the body suffers or rejoices, we all suffer or rejoice. Matthew 28:19-20 commissions us to make disciples, not just of our own body of believers but of all the nations, in order to transform the world into the kingdom of God. Both Paul and the Gospel writer of Matthew had a vision when they wrote. Paul envisioned how disciples should relate to one another; the Gospel writer envisioned inviting all people of all nations to become disciples of Jesus Christ.

Mission and Vision

As important as a vision was to Paul and the Gospel writer, it is apparent in the study of Scripture that their mission of making disciples is what shaped their vision. *Mission* defines why we exist; it is what we do; it is the business we are in. Our mission is what gives shape, form, and boundaries to our task. The mission is the framework that holds the vision. *Vision* is the picture inside the frame. To be effective, a vision must be clear and strong enough to pull people into the future. And a vision must be shared and communicated in order to be realized.

When Jesus' disciples were called, their mission was to follow Jesus, but their vision was to be fishers of people, inviting others to follow Jesus. Martin Luther King, Jr's mission was integration and civil rights, but his vision was all people living together in love.

Our Christian mission is to make disciples. If we are to strengthen discipleship among youth and young adults, we need a big vision: a vision that looks beyond their youth and young-adults years into their middle years and old age. We need a vision that provides opportunities to shape a lifelong commitment to discipleship.

What Is System Thinking?

Too often, people spend their time thinking of a quick fix to problems. However, as soon as one problem has been taken care of, another problem comes along. Sometimes the way the first problem was solved may be the cause of a new problem. System thinking is a lens through which we can look at our ministry with youth and young adults. System thinking requires us to look at the whole, not just at bits and pieces. So, when we do system thinking in youth and young-adult ministries, we take into account the overall church. It is important to remember, though, that system thinking and planning are results oriented. A system can do only what it is designed to do. For example, a system designed to get someone to Paris, Tennessee, is not the same system that is needed to get that person to Paris, France.

Disciple-Making Is a System

A system is an interdependent group of people, processes, functions, and activities that work together for a common aim. When Paul wrote about one body with many parts, he described the body as such a system. Paul wanted all the parts of the body to work in harmony with other parts, each part being aware of the contribution it makes to the whole. For Paul, the core of this system thinking was to move a church from internal quarreling to transforming love for one another. Paul knew what business he was in.

Historically, the church has been a system. It is a system designed to reach people, receive them into the fellowship of the church, relate them to God, nurture them in discipleship, and then send them out into the world to live as disciples, extending the reach of the church.

What Does a Discipleship System Look Like?

In the life and ministry of Jesus, we can discover some key elements that must be present in a discipleship system.

First and foremost, *Jesus went to the people.* He risked his reputation to fulfill his mission with the poor, the rich, the hungry, and the abused.

Second, *Jesus invited people to become disciples.* Jesus took the time to know the people he was inviting. Some whom Jesus invited were called by name: Zacchaeus (Luke 19:5) and Simon, the Pharisee (Luke 7:40). Others were called when Jesus had observed them or

Think for a Moment

How will disciple-making of youth and young adults impact and support the mission and vision of your church?

Think for a Moment

As a leader of youth and young adults, you must know the business you are in.

noticed their work: Nathanael (John 1:47-48) and Nicodemus (John 3:1). And then there was the Samaritan woman, whose past Jesus knew in detail (John 4:16-19).

Third, *Jesus' invitation required a person to physically move*: "Come and follow me." Jesus was asking each person to make a commitment to a lifetime of spiritual growth and service. One who could not make the commitment to follow Jesus "went away grieving, for he had many possessions" (Matthew 19:20-22).

Fourth, *Jesus immediately began to teach his disciples.* He taught in the language of the people. He illustrated his teachings in a way that was understandable: through stories, through illustrations from everyday life, and through familiar sayings.

Lastly, *Jesus made it clear that discipleship involves leaving the old life behind* to make a commitment to a new life (Luke 14:25-33).

Discipleship is invitational.

Discipleship is all about relationships.

Understanding Youth and Young Adults

Maslow's pyramid of human needs—safety, belonging, participation, acceptance, and affirmation—outlines how relationships develop. Over the years, much of the language of Maslow's pyramid has changed, and the needs have been broken into segments, but the basics of Maslow's ideas remain the same. For example, in order to develop relationships, certain critical needs have to be met first: security, praise, and self-esteem. Referring to Maslow, these needs can be broken down into safety and belonging (security), participation (praise), and acceptance and affirmation (self-esteem). In order to build relationships, it is also essential to meet the need for identity; that is, the need for knowing who I am: Who am I? Who are the significant people in my life? Who loves me? Who is God?

Congregations need to embrace youth and young adults where they are and assist them in developing an awareness of who they are and how to discern life needs. Congregations need to develop and build a variety of opportunities, both inside and outside the walls of the church, to allow those who participate

- to be introduced to the faith;
- to learn about faith traditions, including their own;
- to claim the faith as their own and bridge it with everyday life;
- to act out the faith in the church, community, and world.

Need for Self-Actualization (to create, contribute, develop)

Esteem Needs (be respected and self-respect)

Love and Belongingness Needs (feel accepted, loved by others; need to be with others rather than alone)

Safety Needs (feel safe from present or future harm or threat; stable, predictable environment, free from anxiety and chaos)

Physiological Needs (satisfy basic needs: hunger, thirst, oxygen, sleep, elimination, sex)

Abram Maslow's Hierarchy of Human Needs (1968)

Creating a discipleship system is more about people than about programs, more about relationships than about religion, more about Christ than about creeds, more about choices than about compromises, and more about opportunities for life-changing personal faith than about shallow religious traditions.

Disciple-making must include opportunities for
- group building that leads to a Christian caring community;
- study (content) that assists people in learning about the Christian faith;
- opportunities that enable people to reach out to others.

Without these, the community becomes just another group.

Ways People Enter Into Discipleship

How do youth and young adults come to us? Many are cautious, not sure this is the place they need to be. Others are curious, wanting to know more. Some are committed and show up for everything. Still others have reached a level of spiritual maturity that invites stretching and going deeper into discipleship. And finally, there are those who know where they are on their journey and invite others to join them. It is the task of a leader to provide opportunities that encourage and support movement through these stages toward deeper spiritual growth. With each stage there is a ministry style that can help draw people through the stages toward a full and complete relationship with God through Christ.

Stage of Discipleship	Helpful Ministry Style
Cautious • Suspicious • Uncomfortable • Unfamiliar • Unsure about visiting or letting defenses down	**Gateway** • Know their name • Introduce them to others • Have moderate but purposeful programs • Do not put them on the spot
Curious • Interested in knowing more • Have not engaged with the group • Not convinced the Christian life is for them	**Stand Alone** • Satisfy curiosity • Relate to other Christians • Offer short-term service opportunities
Committed • Committed to group and growth but not to a personal relationship with Christ • Not disciplined in faith growth	**Ongoing** • Longer-term study opportunities • Opportunities for a decision for Christ • Opportunities for service
Professing • Committed to having Christ at center of life • Aware of God's presence • Think that church programs are not religious enough	**Outreach** • Focus on disciplines of the faith and living as members of the body of Christ • Encourage to take leadership roles
Inviting • Deeply committed • Seek to help others into discipleship • Focus on living their faith	**Teach, Reach, Receive** • Shared strategies for reaching others • Advanced leadership training • Significant leadership roles

The process of coming into and growing in discipleship is fundamentally a process of participation. When people participate in communities that know God's love, express God's love, and live a life reflective of God's love, they desire to be drawn into that fellowship/community of people as a participant.

Practices of Discipleship

Throughout the history of the Christian church, some practices have remained constant in disciple-making. "Practices are the constitutive acts of a community that both identify us as, and form us into, people who belong to that community. Christian practices mark us as and make us into Jesus' followers."[1] In *The Godbearing Life,* Kenda Creasy Dean and Ron Foster list thirty-eight examples of Christian practices. The list has examples of at least nine broader practices that have been consistent throughout the history of the church in forming disciples:

- *Worship:* praising and thanking God, hearing God's Word preached, receiving the sacraments;
- *Bible Study:* reading/studying/interpreting/relating to our life;
- *Christian Conferencing:* being in groups where we can listen to and talk to one another about our understanding of how we are living in relationship to following Christ;
- *Prayer:* both together and by ourselves, in all times and in all places;
- *Mutual Support:* bearing one another's burdens in a noncondemning way;
- *Outreach/Mission:* specific opportunities for being in service;
- *Sharing Gifts:* not just financial but also talents, in a generous way;
- *Hospitality:* caring not only for our own but also for the stranger we meet;
- *Social Action:* working to carry out God's will in all the world.

The following chart combines these nine Christian practices with the stages of discipleship in the chart on page 130 to help you evaluate your discipleship system with youth and young adults. Use this chart to create a disciple-making system for each of the stages in which you will be engaging youth and young adults. As you work through the practices and stages, ask yourself these questions:

1. Does everyone know the names of all the members of the group?
2. Is there a sense that those who come belong here?
3. Can God be experienced here?
4. Are there opportunities for people to hear God calling them?
5. Are people invited to move to deeper levels of commitment?
6. Is there evidence of transformation: people moving into a fuller life in Christ?

	Cautious	Curious	Committed	Professing	Inviting
Worship					
Bible Study					
Christian Conferencing					
Prayer					
Mutual Support					
Outreach/ Mission					
Sharing Gifts					
Hospitality					
Social Action					

We live in an age when there are plenty of secular organizations who provide fun events, dynamic recreation leaders, and good moral instruction. But it is only in the church where youth and young adults can be awakened to the liberating presence of God that leads to a life of discipleship.

Endnote
1 From *The Godbearing Life: The Art of Soul-Tending for Youth Ministry.* Copyright © 1998 by Kenda Creasy Dean and Ron Foster. Used by permission of Upper Room Books.

Millennials and Worship

Craig Kennet Miller

For years, congregations have debated the merits of contemporary versus traditional worship. On one side are those who say we must remember the traditions of the faith; on the other are those who say we must have praise bands and use the music of today to attract younger people. As congregations seek to attract Millennials, they are finding that both sides are important. Millennials are attracted to an experience that keeps them in touch with the traditions of the faith while helping them live today.

In North American culture, we see a dramatic change from the religion of the 1950's to the way people view religion today. In the 1950's, people lived out of a secular versus religious mindset. There was the world of the church and the world of the secular society. This mindset affected worship in these three ways:

1. People joined a church because they agreed with a set of beliefs. They affiliated with a particular denomination because of its stance on the Bible, baptism, Communion, and social issues. Worship revolved around remembering the beliefs, so the affirmation of faith and The Lord's Prayer were critical elements that helped people remember key beliefs.
2. Big band, jazz, and rock 'n' roll music were categorized as secular, while classical, gospel, and hymns were appropriate in church. Instrumentation followed suit, with some instruments, such as drums and electric guitars, being clearly defined as secular.
3. Ninety-six percent of people claimed a religious affiliation, so the goal of evangelism was to move people from non-participation to membership.

Today, people no longer live out of that same mindset. Instead of wanting to be part of a religion, they are interested in exploring their spirituality. Spirituality used to be the domain of the church, but now spirituality is talked about in business, education, health, sports, and even government. All talk about the value of a higher power connects a person to all aspects of life. As a result, rather than focusing on beliefs, worship that speaks to people today offers an experience of the grace of God through which they come to know the person and work of Jesus Christ. Worship is affected by this in three ways:

1. The use of traditional elements, such as the affirmation of faith and The Lord's Prayer, are for teaching rather than for remembering. Rather than assuming that people know the beliefs and traditions of the faith, use sacraments, prayers, and liturgies to move people into the experience of worship. Rather than an end in themselves, they enable worshipers to make a connection with God.

2. Any style of music is acceptable when done well. Classical as well as rock has its place in worship when it invites people to worship God. A wide variety of musical instruments, from organ to drums, enhances the worship experience.

3. The goal of evangelism is discipleship. Rather than focusing on membership, people see themselves on a spiritual journey. Their question is, How does being a Christian shape spiritual life and enable us to become whole? How do we live our faith outside the bounds of the church? How does a relationship with Jesus Christ affect our relationships with family, friends, coworkers, and those who are outside of the faith?

As we create worship for Millennials, these changes in the wider culture shape the focus of a congregation's worship life in several ways. First, Millennials do not necessarily want their own worship service. Instead, they want to be invited to be leaders in worship. To attract Millennials, congregations need to have Millennials reading Scripture, singing in choirs, playing musical instruments, or ushering. When other Millennials see people like themselves involved in the service, they feel that this place is for them.

Second, Millennials are not interested in the contemporary versus traditional debate. Instead, they like an eclectic use of rituals, prayers, and music styles in worship. For them, having a time of silent prayer is an alternative to the high-powered, go-go-go lifestyle of the electronic culture. Finding a place and a time to experience the peace of God is a felt need for Millennials.

Third, worship is an experience of the grace of God. Through worship, people are offered an opportunity to be transformed through an encounter with the living Christ. Through singing, praying, hearing the Word of God, and proclamation, Millennials are called to renewal of mind, body, and spirit as they hear God's call for their lives.

As congregations develop experience-based worship that speaks to the needs of Millennials, the worship matrix can be a great tool to help them shape the worship experience. By using the worship matrix, a worship team can identify the elements of worship that best speak to the group for whom this worship experience is being created. These are basic elements of a worship experience:

- **Sacraments:** Baptism and Communion
- **Historic Hymns:** Historic hymns that help worshipers remember the faith of those who came before
- **Creeds and Prayers:** Prayers like The Lord's Prayer or creeds like the Apostles' Creed unite across time and across generations.

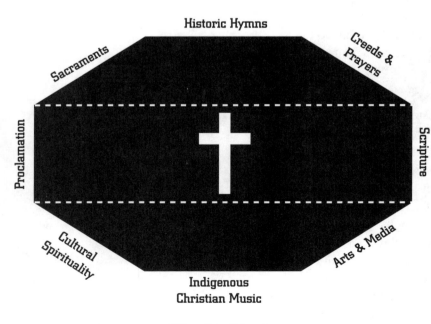

Worship Matrix

Historic Hymns

Creeds & Prayers

Sacraments

Proclamation

Scripture

Cultural Spirituality

Arts & Media

Indigenous Christian Music

- **Scripture:** Scripture, the focal point of the worship experience, helps identify the theme and question for the day.
- **Arts & Media:** A wide variety of arts invites participants into the heart of worship. Drama, music, graphics, video clips, even silence can touch participants with a new insight in their relationship to God.
- **Indigenous Christian Music:** Both the kind of music and the way it is presented are critical for relating to the world of Millennials. Most Millennials enjoy an eclectic mix of music, from classical to pop, from rock to Latin, from hip-hop to country. The key is to identify what style of presentation and instrumentation will be the norm. For example, a congregation may decide the piano and organ are the norm. Most congregational singing and music from soloists and choirs will be accompanied by these two classical instruments. For a different worship experience, this same congregation may decide that the norm will be keyboard, guitars, and drums.

  Once the norm is identified, worship leaders can add additional instruments, such as a flute or a fiddle, to add a different feel to the basic instrumentation that enhances a particular song. A creative addition of musical instruments allows a wide variety of music styles while the basic norm gives continuity from week to week.
- **Cultural Spirituality:** The use of popular songs, video clips, poems, and stories taps into what the wider culture is saying about relating to God. Typically, the use of cultural spirituality helps focus worshipers on the question or issue for that day.
- **Proclamation:** Preaching that speaks to Millennials is relational and visionary. It helps participants see how God is in relationship with them through Jesus Christ. It is not afraid to tackle the tough issues of the day, and it shows how Jesus transforms people's lives. It focuses on the call to be in ministry for and with others and leaves room for the power of the Holy Spirit to reveal God's will for their lives.

Once a worship team identifies the elements that will be used each week, they can focus on developing each worship service with variety and meaning. Let us say that a congregation offers a worship experience at nine on Sunday mornings with the following norms:

9:00 a.m. Worship Experience
Indigenous Music: Christian contemporary
Music Instrumentation: Piano and acoustic guitar
Call to worship followed by three songs
Communion
Lord's Prayer
Scripture
Message
Offering
Closing song

As the worship team prepares for a particular worship experience, they may do something such as this:

First Sunday in February	Second Sunday in February
Music instrumentation: piano, guitar, violin, cello	Music instrumentation: piano, guitar, drums, bass
Call to worship	Call to worship
Three praise songs	Three praise songs
Lord's Prayer	Communion
Video Clip	Scripture
Scripture	Drama
Message	Message
Offering	Offering
Anthem	Lord's Prayer
Communion	Solo
Closing song	Closing song

As you compare the two experiences, you find that while both start the same and help establish the feel for the service, the additional musical instruments, the different elements, and the order create two different experiences. The beauty of this is that participants in both worship experiences feel a continuity from one week to the next while the variety helps keep the worship experience new and engaging. As you create worship for Millennials, the use of traditional worship practices offered in a new way keeps interest and helps them grow in their spiritual formation.

As congregations develop experience-based worship for Millennials, it is important to keep in mind these basic principles:

1. Worship is drama. The flow of worship is like a one-act play. How do the elements of worship shape an experience that truly causes the worshipers to make a connection with God?
2. Everything that happens in worship is part of the message. From the decorations on the altar to the concluding benediction, everything feeds into the overall theme of the day.
3. Everything is media. From the pews or chairs to the worship bulletin or PowerPoint slide, everything is a communication device.
4. Digital media is just a tool. Many congregations think that in order to reach Millennials, they must use video projectors, computers, and video clips. While these things can enhance the ability to communicate, they are not the whole answer. In fact, the overuse of digital media can actually turn Millennials off. What does speak to Millennials is a community of faith that authentically lives out its faith. What does touch Millennials are people who care, who pray, who go out of their way to make Millennials feel like they are welcome and that this is their church.

Reinventing the Sunday School

Carol F. Krau

s a child in the 1950's, I grew up singing "Jesus Wants Me for a Sunbeam" and "I Will Make You Fishers of Men." My teachers held competitions that awarded prizes for bringing a Bible to Sunday school, bringing a friend to church, and memorizing Scripture. We received perfect attendance pins, and some of us had chests full of bars that testified to years of participation. We sat around a table coloring pictures of Jesus and taking turns reading the Bible story for the day. Naturally, all this took place on Sunday morning. They did not name it Sunday school for nothing.

While your experience may have differed from mine, in many congregations the above picture represents the Sunday schools built by the GI Generation in the years following World War II. As these civic-minded adults bought the first televisions, organized Scout troops, and started new businesses, they also built new buildings to hold the growing number of children coming through the doors of their churches. They spent time and money on programs that would encourage their children to be loyal members of churches that later became The United Methodist Church.

However, they were disappointed. As Baby Boomers matured, they rebelled against authority, challenged the status quo, and ignored the institutions that had been so carefully created by their parents. By the mid-1960's, the birth rate was declining. By the mid-1970's, the Sunday school began to feel the effects of these trends.

In the years since 1975, total church school membership has dropped from 4,654,211 to 3,660, 275 in 1998 (approximately twenty-one percent). The number of children (birth through sixth grade) in our Sunday schools has dropped from 1,487,606 in 1975 to 1,070,852 in 1998 (approximately twenty-eight percent).

Of course, the decline in Sunday school enrollment is more than a result of changing demographics. Other factors include children who alternate weekends between parents, school activities, work responsibilities, and entertainment opportunities scheduled for Sunday. Families expect to have alternatives for worship, study, fellowship, and service. They choose the option that most closely matches their time schedule, interests, and faith maturity.

I think it is fairly safe to say that business as usual no longer works. If you ask me, it is past time for our congregational leaders to reinvent the Sunday school. It is time to clarify exactly what we are trying to accomplish and then determine what particular structures will help us accomplish our aim.

DemoFacts

In 1975, church school membership was 4,654,211. By 1998, it had dropped twenty-one percent to 3,660,275.

Our Aim

The mission of the church is to make disciples of Jesus Christ. In the past, there was an unspoken analogy between discipleship and membership. If we attended Sunday school and worship, contributed money, and served in some capacity within the congregation (usher, committee member, and so forth), then we were good members. Oops! I meant disciples. Well, I really meant members. Our mental model was that of membership. The church was an organization that one could choose to provide support for and receive benefits from upon becoming a member.

As we shift our mental model from membership to discipleship, we realize that what we do together may be radically different from the past. Gone are the days of providing services in return for loyalty. Now it is time to prepare our children to experience God's presence and live together as God's people, serving the world in Jesus' name.

I would like to suggest that there are two primary ways in which we can engage in this kind of preparation. The first is corporate worship. (For more ideas related to worship, check out the article "Millennials and Worship," on pages 133–36 in this book.) The second is through a variety of small groups.

In some congregations, small groups will continue to include Sunday school. As long as children are experiencing God and learning to live as God's people, that is great. In many places, however, congregations need to experiment with small-group ministry structures that are just emerging or possibly have not been tried yet. As we consider how to structure these settings, we need to be sure to include the components that most effectively shape our Christian identity and mission. Some of these components are

- studying Scripture;
- praying;
- experiencing a community of Christian friends, teachers, and mentors;
- naming our experiences of God;
- reflecting on the connections between God's story and our individual and corporate stories;
- identifying and developing the gifts we have to offer our community;
- participating in ministry to others;
- finding support for ongoing transformation into the image of Christ.

One example of how congregations have been experimenting with new structures is the rotation model for Sunday school. In this model, one biblical story is explored through a variety of methods over a course of several weeks. Each teaching method has its own location, and small groups of children rotate through the different methods for exploring the story. The children experience one method each week. After a few weeks they have experienced the story in several different ways.

According to Neil MacQueen, coauthor of *Workshop Rotation: A New Model for Sunday School,* several thousand congregations use some form of the rotation model. In addition, MacQueen estimates that there are approximately five thousand congregations teaching with computers to some extent in their ministries with children. The number of churches using the rotation model and the number of churches teaching with computers are both growing at about twenty percent a year.

R.E.A.C.H. Through Small Groups

Small-group opportunities for the Millennial Generation need to include these emphases:

Relationships
Experience
Application
Contribution
Holistic

Relationships—This generation needs solid relationships with adults, with their peers, and with God. Young people need adults who model respect, openness, and faith. They need a dependable peer group that provides a supportive community for learning and growing. Most of all, they need a relationship with God through Jesus Christ. They need practices, stories, symbols, and songs that help them discover the reality of God in their lives.

Experience—Relationships may benefit from information, but at heart they are experiential. We have relationships with one another as we talk, play, work, study, and worship together. We learn best when we are immersed in an experience. Young people are not asking for information about God; they have a deep yearning to experience God's presence. Any small group must consider how to foster such an experience.

Application—In our fast-paced world, we have little time to spend on activities that provide no benefits. If you want young people to participate in your small groups, those groups will need to have a direct application to their lives. Group activities must be relevant and must address the real-life needs of the group members.

Contribution—Young people want to make a contribution in this world, so small groups should help them discover their natural gifts and abilities. Together, young people should use their gifts for the benefit of the congregation and the community. As they share their lives with others, they will develop a sense of connection, self-worth, and appreciation for life.

Holistic—Finally, small groups need to be holistic in nature. Group experiences should speak to the mind, body, and spirit. The old schooling model for Christian education is not adequate for forming Christian disciples. We must create settings that challenge our minds, engage our emotions, and use our bodies.

As you experiment with small-group ministries with children, remember that not every group will meet the needs of every child. You will need to provide a variety of small groups that emphasize the various components of discipleship formation. And do not be afraid of

Pointers for Parents

- Talk to your children about your experience of God. Use simple words. Focus on sharing your experience, remembering that your child may experience God differently.

- Read Bible stories to your child. Demonstrate that the Bible is an important book to you.

- Participate with your child in some form of service. Visit a nursing home, serve a meal at a homeless shelter, participate in a CROP Walk or other fundraiser for hunger or other community concerns.

- Use a resource such as *FaithTalk* cards (Augsburg Youth and Family Institute, 877-239-2492 or www.youthfamilyinstitute.com). These work with children and youth and can be played as a game at home or in the car. On each card is something to talk about related to faith, family memories, values, and deeds of service. Make your own cards, and take out one card each week for a topic of discussion at a family meal.

- Make church education a family priority. As children and youth see parents involved in study, they are more likely to continue participating in Sunday school, Bible study, or other small groups.

What Your Church Can Do

- Review the list of components for small-group ministries (page 138) and the emphases for small groups (page 139). What would you add? How would you describe the necessary elements in forming Christian disciples? Think about the ways in which these components and characteristics are evident in your ministry with young people. Consider which ones are missing or need to be strengthened.

- Use Advent, Lent, or the summer to try out a new model for ministry, such as the rotation model. (See the bibliography for resources in this and other ministry models. Also visit the websites www.rotation.org and www.sundaysoftware.com.)

- Partner with schools and other community organizations to create safe settings for children to learn, play, and serve.

- Try an intergenerational format. Involve children and their parents in study together using the material in *FaithHome,* by MaryJane Pierce Norton, Debra Ball-Kilbourne, Dan Solomon, and Joy Solomon (Abingdon Press, October 1997). Or use one of the forty-five lessons in *Side by Side: Families Learning and Living the Faith Together,* by Delia Halverson (Abingdon Press, 2002), to have adults and children learn and work together.

- Keep in contact, through an online Bible study, with college students, people in the service, or those who have moved.

failure. If something does not work, talk about why it did not, make the necessary changes, and try again.

The Millennials are waiting for us to step up to the plate. God grant us the wisdom and courage to create settings in which these precious children and young adults can experience God's presence and live as God's people.

Faith Passage

Reginald Blount

00000—1982/1999—00000

Rite of Passage

When was the first time you realized you were an adult?

- When you graduated from high school?
- When you got your driver's license?
- When you started paying your own bills?
- When you decided it was time to move out on your own?
- When you got married?
- When you started having children?
- When a young person called you Mr. or Ms.?

For some, adulthood became reality at eighteen; for others, it did not become real until forty. How do we know when adulthood has finally arrived? Allow me to offer a bold, controversial, indicting statement: North American society (in particular, the United States) has failed its youth. I believe one of our greatest failures in society, and in the church, is not offering our youth clear markers that let them know when they have transitioned from adolescence to adulthood.

Instead, we offer our youth mixed messages. They can vote and smoke cigarettes at eighteen, but they cannot drink alcohol until age twenty-one. The legal age to drive a vehicle, the legal age of consent, and the legal age to marry vary from state to state. Adulthood status in our judicial system is predicated on the type of crime committed.

What clear markers do we offer youth on the journey to adulthood that alert them they have arrived? Those who study adolescent development are clear that this is a life stage of great change. Young people are changing mentally, physically, and spiritually. They are trying to make sense of who they are, where they fit, and what their purpose is in life. They are seeking independence not so much from adult control but from adults' view of them as children. They are seeking affirmation of the changes that are taking place in their bodies, thoughts, and spirits. They are desiring to be taken seriously as emerging adults. The problem facing both society and the church is that there are no rituals that celebrate the end of childhood, the training period of adolescence, and the commencement of adulthood.

The church has a responsibly, an obligation, to offer young people the appropriate markers that let them know when they have made the transition from adolescence to adulthood. Churches can fulfill this obligation by offering youth a faith-forming rite of passage that helps them "put an end to childish ways" (1 Corinthians 13:11) and become faith-filled, responsible citizens of God's kingdom.

There are normally three stages to a rites-of-passage process:

- a separation stage, when the initiates are physically taken away from their community;
- an initiation stage, when extensive training is conducted on what it means to be a responsive and responsible member of the community;
- a reincorporation stage, when the initiate is welcomed back into the community as an adult and granted rights, privileges, and responsibilities of an adult in the community.

How do we develop a rite-of-passage model that takes seriously the faith formation of our youth? For a number of years now, rites-of-passage programs have been instituted in a number of African-American churches. *Young Lions: Christian Rites of Passage for African American Young Men* (Abingdon Press, 2001) offers a model for providing young men a faith passage from adolescence to adulthood. You have to know your faith community to know which pattern or model works best for you. Here are some thoughts on how to take seriously the three stages (separation, initiation, and reincorporation) as you consider fashioning a rites-of-passage program for your faith community.

Separation

Separation is key because it takes young people away from their community for a while and out of their comfort zone. It provides them with an opportunity to explore who they are and who they are becoming without the distractions of familiar surroundings. For separation to be effective, it needs to be for some extended period of time. Since it is impossible to take youth away for months or weeks at a time, weekend retreats, overnight lock-ins, summer camp, and mission trips are ideal opportunities to be incorporated into a rites-of-passage model.

Another level of separation needs to take place that requires a change in mindset, a shift in paradigm, particularly in the minds of adults. When youth are about twelve or thirteen, we, as adults, must make a conscious shift from viewing our young people as children to viewing them as adults-in-training. The myth is that when young people reach adolescence, they desire to separate from their parents or other authority figures. That is not true. What young people desire is to be separated from being viewed and treated as a child. Young people welcome guidance and crave mentoring. What they desire is recognition, appreciation, and celebration that they are changing, that they are growing up. We must find ways to honor their growing up. We can do that by intentionally shifting how we view them and begin seeing them not as children but as adults-in-training.

Initiation

Proverbs 22:6 says: "Train children in the right way, and when old, they will not stray." I realize that this proverb was key to my moral and ethical development. I learned the Ten Commandments, and I learned my faith community's understanding of God's do's and don'ts (more don'ts than do's). I learned tradition and rituals and about God. But I must confess that I learned little about what it means to be in

Pointers for Parents

When your child reaches twelve or thirteen, throw a big celebration marking the turning point from childhood to adult-in-training (similar to Jewish bar/bat mitzvah). Begin to help your child discover his or her God-given gifts and talents and ways to share these gifts with his or her faith community.

relationship with God, what it means to experience God. I believe at the heart of a youth's initiation should be developing a deeper, closer, more intimate relationship with God, as well as a caring love of neighbor and a healthy love of self. The time when youth are trying to make sense of independence and intimacy becomes an excellent opportunity to nurture youth in their relationship with God and their responsibility to care for others. What would it mean to initiate, train, equip, or provide guidance to youth in the way that they should go (should journey with God, should draw closer to God and God's creation) so that when they are old, they will not depart from the journey? We can do it if our initiation takes seriously culture, context, and content.

Culture. Part of my understanding of my role as a pastor, as a teacher, and as a preacher of the good news is that I must truly know my audience. As a pastor, I must know my congregation. As a teacher, I must be a student of my students. As a preacher, it is important that I know who I am preaching to. Many of us say we know youth; we feel confident speaking for them and making sweeping determinations about what is best for them. But the truth is that many of us do not know the lives our youth live on a day-to-day basis. Many of us are not in tune with the culture of youth today. We have created a climate in our society that makes it easy to demonize youth, especially youth in our cities, without ever getting to know their reality.

It is important that we realize that youth culture is not monolithic; it takes on various dimensions. Youth culture of suburbia and the youth culture of the inner city are different. Youth culture of a rural environment and the youth culture of an urban city are different. We must become students of the culture our youth live in and navigate. The best learning we will ever receive is what we gain by simply sitting down and talking with youth. They will discuss their world with us if they believe we are truly interested in hearing about it. We are taught that effective ministry takes place when we are able to meet people where they are and at their point of need. That understanding becomes critical as we shape a viable faith passage for youth.

Context. For the initiation stage to be effective, the right kind of context, the right kind of environment, must be in place. It must

- provide interested and caring adults willing to journey with youth. They must be mentors and spiritual guides so that they can help youth wrestle with tough questions and complicated life issues.
- have high expectations of youth and see them as capable theologians, able to reflect critically on faith, tradition, and relationship with God. We need adults who are willing to allow youth the space to doubt, question, and reclaim their faith for themselves.
- provide help in understanding what it means to be in community, including their responsibility to that community. They need help understanding that their relationship with God is also connected to what they do with and for others.
- provide room for youth to make mistakes and model a balance between accountability and grace.
- provide safe spaces for youth, physically, mentally, and emotionally.

Content. The curriculum of any initiating stage should be transformative and liberating and should be geared toward setting youth free, free to be children of God and free to be cocreators with God. Many competing factors try to hold our youth in bondage: poverty, gangs, sex, drugs, peer pressure, unrealistic expectations. The curriculum of the initiating stage should provide the tools for youth to break free and transcend those barriers that keep them from becoming all that God desires for them to be. The curriculum should

- provide a firm foundation in the faith. It should share the faith community's understanding of who God is, as well as its history, doctrines, traditions, and rituals.
- provide opportunities for transformation. It should aid youth in claiming meaning, identity, purpose, and worth as a child of God and as cocreator with God.
- provide opportunities to put their faith into action by showing love for God and neighbor.

Reincorporation

When it is all said and done, how will we welcome young people back into community? What role will they play? What responsibilities will they be given? What space will be made for the gifts they have to share with the faith community? How will they be continually nurtured? These are the questions each faith community takes seriously as they answer the call to help young people make a faithful transition from adolescence to adulthood.

Here are a few suggestions:

- Provide a meaningful ritual at the conclusion of the rites-of-passage process that celebrates the successful completion.
- Provide a significant role in the life of the faith community for the newly initiated adult.
- Provide opportunities to participate in the leadership and decision making taking place in the life of the faith community.
- Provide opportunities for their voices to be heard and affirmed.
- Provide opportunities for continued mentoring and nurturing as they begin to encounter the many challenges of adulthood.

A person should not have to wait until age forty to realize he or she has reached adulthood. The church can be instrumental in helping youth "put an end to childish ways" and make a meaningful faith passage toward becoming a responsible citizen of God's kingdom.

What Your Church Can Do

Provide opportunities for youth to have an active role in the leadership and decision making of the church.

Becoming Multiethnic

Victor Quon

Some people might find it difficult to believe that an ethnic church can have racial problems of its own. However, that is just the story of The San Jose Chinese Alliance Church. The church, founded in 1975, had a mission: to reach the unchurched Chinese population of Santa Clara Valley, also known as the Silicon Valley. For its first twenty-three years (through 1998), The San Jose Chinese Alliance Church remained an almost exclusively Chinese ministry. The church had a few blended families and a few people who were of different Asian backgrounds, but the church membership was still well over ninety-five percent Chinese.

While I served as the youth pastor of the church, it became clear to me in 1997 that we were not reaching all the students in the valley—not even all of the Chinese students. An appeal was made to start planting youth groups outside of the church walls, with the intent of reaching more students with the gospel of Jesus Christ. I would like to be able to say that I had noticed that our church had put up our own ethnic barriers and that God had placed it upon my heart to lead our church into becoming a multiethnic ministry, but the truth is that it was not my idea. The reality of a new multiethnic ministry came over time through a movement of the Holy Spirit.

Our original plans called for planting a new youth group on the west side of the valley, where most of our current students lived. Our goal was to get the youth group outside the limits of the church walls. The plan was to reach new students by locating a youth group meeting close to their homes so that they would not have to cross over to the east-side location of the church campus. It sounded like a great idea. But if you have ever seen the Holy Spirit work, you already know what the Spirit of God thinks of strategies based on earthly wisdom.

The group of students who volunteered to plant the first new youth group came not from the west side where we had intended but from the east side of the valley where our church is located. Not only did the students want to plant their group on the east side instead of on the west side but they also wanted to start the group in the church rather than out in the community. Their plan was directly opposed to what we had originally envisioned for our new youth group. But the students noted that our youth ministry was already reaching students on the west side, but hardly any students on the east side were a part of the church. The students also stated that they felt restricted in reaching out only to Chinese students. They wanted to share the gospel with their friends, no matter what their ethnic backgrounds might be. We asked, "What about the location? Won't non-Christian

What Your Church Can Do

Because a new faith community must meet the needs of a new people group, those who are called to minister to the younger Millennial Generation will need to seriously consider creating multiethnic, single-culture faith communities that reflect the current reality of the everyday life of these young people.

NextChurch.Now: Creating New Faith Communities, by Craig Kennet Miller, page 49. © 2000 Discipleship Resources. Used by permission.

DemoFacts

Fifty-five percent of Millennials say they have a close friend of another race.

Millennial Generation Survey, 2002

students be too intimidated to meet at a church?" The students said, "No, the church is the place they expect to see God." I could see my new vision for ministry disappearing quickly, so I immediately interrupted, "Yeah, but...but... You know, you're right!" So much for theological training and grand visions of ministry. The students had it right all along.

During the same time that I was working to create a new youth ministry, the Spirit of God was also moving in the life of our senior pastor, Rev. Abraham Poon. He helped our pastoral staff and church leaders remember that one of the reasons the church purchased the piece of property on which our buildings sat was to evangelize the neighborhood. During the eleven years at our location, we had started a tutoring program and had sponsored a children's program conducted by City Team Ministries. But there was little to show from those programs. Sunday mornings were still very Chinese. Rev. Poon led the church to begin prayer-walking the surrounding neighborhood. We began to seek the Lord's wisdom in knowing how to reach the people living around the church property.

The student leaders who had volunteered to start the new youth group began to meet with two adult volunteers for Bible study, prayer, and planning sessions. By February 1998, they were ready to start. They made flyers and passed them out to friends at school, in workplaces, and in their neighborhoods. We had no idea who was going to come to the first meeting, but we opened the doors of the church chapel on February 10, 1998, and started S.O.U.L. (Shine On Us, Lord) Fellowship. A dinner and program that night was attended by twenty-nine young men and women, most of whom had never set foot inside a church before. Although this was a good beginning, we figured that the numbers would drop in the ensuing weeks, since that is normal for new programs. But each succeeding week, the numbers were either stable or had increased.

What also increased as the group of youth increased was the concern from church parents. The students who regularly came to S.O.U.L. did not appear to be anything like the typical students who came from the church families. Many of the S.O.U.L. students had experienced trouble with the law. They had experimented with drugs and alcohol, came from families that were not strong, and were not star students. Some of the girls had been through abortions. The students in S.O.U.L. dressed differently from the youth in the church families; they had various hair colors; and they had rings in a variety of places on their bodies. The ethnic mix was no longer primarily Chinese. The ethnic mix was such that we called the new group our "Chinese, Filipino, Vietnamese, Cambodian, Hispanic, African-American, Caucasian Youth Group."

Even though S.O.U.L. met on Tuesday nights, when no other group was even near the property, parents were concerned about the impact the new group might have on their church kids. The fear was that the church kids might become like the S.O.U.L. kids. One of the e-mails I received expressing concern went something like this:

In our church we have seldom been prepared or taught to do this kind of outreach program. To see people with their hair dyed in different colors and embracing each other so tightly in public, well, I cannot stand it. I think that whatever that person is doing is saying or reflecting something about his/her own lifestyle. If we as Christians do not have Christian lifestyles or, even worse, start following the world's lifestyle, then we are in deep trouble. Furthermore, can we take the pressure if our own children's behavior and appearance becomes like theirs? Influence goes both ways. Either the non-Christian youth will transform themselves to become Christians because of good examples, or our kids will get contaminated. The chances are equal.

For the next two years, S.O.U.L. continued to flourish. Countless stories of conversions and healings continued to come forth from Tuesday nights. Although some of the church parents were still hesitant, others grew to be supportive of the new youth group. In most cases, the church youth had little trouble accepting the S.O.U.L. students. Camps, retreats, and outreach events gave a number of opportunities for interaction.

Eventually, a number of the S.O.U.L. students came forward for baptism. Their testimonies touched the hearts of all the church members who were in attendance. The transformations in their lives were strong testimonies to how the Spirit of God can change a person's life.

S.O.U.L. no longer meets on Tuesday nights. The church decided that the students in the fellowship had outgrown the youth department. After two years, most of them had moved into their college years, so the ministry was transitioned to the Pastor for College and Young Adults. S.O.U.L. now meets as a weekly worship service on Sunday afternoons and tries to reach the multicultural community that lives around the church. The ministry team that plans the service is made up of a mixture of traditional church members and students who have grown up as Christians in S.O.U.L. Fellowship.

Millennial Voices

"I made friends with him, seeing the color of his skin as one of the myriad differences that makes us all unique. Thus I never saw anyone as superior or inferior based on outward appearance."

Millennial Generation Survey, 2002

To provide a more well-rounded ministry at the S.O.U.L. service, the church recently hired an Hispanic-American couple and a Caucasian worship leader. It was not too long ago that it would have been unusual to have a non-Chinese person visit the church office. Now, familiar visitors of various ethnic backgrounds drop by with regularity. The church has not only visitors of various backgrounds but also church staff and members from various backgrounds.

In order for S.O.U.L. to have become such a prominent feature of our church's life, a number of people had to respond to God's prompting. God began by giving me the vision to plant youth groups; God imparted a desire to the east-side church students to reach their peers; God moved in the lives of adult volunteers to provide the weekly programming; God grew one of the S.O.U.L. students to take a prominent role in preaching and evangelism; and God put the group under a senior pastor who was not afraid to give his blessing for the group to exist within the church's youth program. Now God has given a new shepherd in our Pastor for College and Young Adults to lead S.O.U.L. into a new chapter of ministry.

The fears of some of our church parents have actually come true. Our church kids have become like the S.O.U.L. students. We have become more expressive in worship, more fervent in prayer, and more passionate about evangelism. S.O.U.L. Fellowship has taught our church how to expand our understanding of the Great Commission. We no longer exist just to make disciples among the Chinese. Our vision now includes all the nations of the world. Our church is functioning more biblically than at any other time in our history.

One final change in our church needs to be mentioned. On February 27, 2000, by unanimous congregational vote, the church changed its name from The San Jose *Chinese* Alliance Church to The San Jose *Christian* Alliance Church.

The Pastor's Role With Millennials

Rob Weber

What is the role of the pastor in ordering the life of the congregation for effective ministry with Millennials? Two ideas come to mind: get connected and facilitate bridge building.

Get Connected

I visited a church recently and observed the children's time during the worship service. I was happy to see the focused time provided with the children, but the way the time was structured did not match the intended emphasis of ministry with children. The preacher, in his flowing black robe, called the children forward to sit on the floor at the base of the five-foot-high chancel platform. He then stood above them on the platform and spoke down to them. The children's message was good, but I could not help looking at the preacher from the perspective of the children: a distant giant towering above them speaking the word of the Lord.

In his book *The Spectacle of Worship in a Wired World,* Tex Sample discusses the idea of Jesus as the one who came to dwell with God's people. He refers to the word that is usually translated as "dwelt," as in "he dwelt among us." The translation that he offers for this word is "to pitch a tent." The model, then, for Jesus' ministry in the world was being one who pitched his tent. In other words, Jesus got connected with those he was trying to reach. This same model is important when considering the pastor's or teacher's role in ministering with Millennial children, youth, or young adults.

What does it mean to get connected with Millennials? Connection involves being real, being relational, being genuinely interested in what is interesting to the Millennials and being willing to learn about life in their world.

I am the father of a Millennial. I find that the more time I spend with him, listening and learning, the better able I am to understand him and the lives of the other Millennials in our congregation. My natural tendency might be to say, "Let's go throw the baseball together," which is one of the things I enjoyed doing with my father. However, I have found that the relationship with my son deepens when I enter into some of the things in his world that would not necessarily be what I would have chosen to do. I will not lie. I do not find it a great sacrifice to play Nintendo, learn a new computer game, or watch cartoons with my son. Sometimes I would rather be doing something else, but in this interaction and in pitching my tent in his world of electronic media adventure and stories, my son and I gain a common language and learn from each other.

 **DemoFacts**

How often do you go to religious services?

56%	Weekly
14%	Yearly
13%	Never
9%	Twice a month
8%	Monthly

Millennial Generation Survey, 2002

These times spent with my son not only help build my relationship with him but also strengthen my ability to communicate with other Millennials, and with their Postmodern parents, in new ways.

While the older members of the congregation might be somewhat confused when I use a sermon illustration from the digitally animated cartoon *Beast Wars,* the Millennials feel recognized, and a connection is made. Once, after a sermon that included an illustration from a cartoon, a parent came to me and said, "I didn't know where you were going when you started talking about *Beast Wars* in the sermon. I have to admit that I was beginning to feel a little perturbed. But then I looked at my ten-year-old, who was listening as intently as I have ever seen him listen in church. That story was not the only thing he heard. When we got in the car on the way home, he started to ask all kinds of questions about the ideas you shared in the rest of the sermon. We had one of the best discussions about faith we have ever had. Thank you." When speaking to farmers and rural agrarians of the first century A.D., Jesus spoke of seeds and soils because that was what the people knew. Is it possible that the same model of incarnational communication carries forward into the Millennial world?

It is not enough, however, for a pastor to be connected with the language and lives of Millennials. A pastor also bears the primary responsibility for being a champion of the value of facilitating intergenerational connectedness with all generations. With the pastor's example, perhaps other influential adults in the congregation will be inspired to get connected with the Millennials and find ways that they can be in ministry together.

Facilitating Intergenerational Bridge Building

Life in Louisiana has taught me a few things. One of them is the process of preparing seafood gumbo. When cooking gumbo, many different ingredients are used. The combination of the flavors provides the richness and the complexity of the dish. If the chef were to cook all of the ingredients separately and then stir them together just before serving, the result would be less than appealing. An important part of the process is the interaction of the ingredients as they cook.

First, the chef makes a roux (flour and butter cooked together until brown), which serves as the base for the interaction of the flavors. The onions and peppers flavor the crab and the shrimp, while the shrimp and crab flavor the onions and peppers.

The same process used to make flavorful seafood gumbo is also important in planning for age-level programming. In the area of program development, it has long been the norm to use age-level segmentation. Division by age level is natural, since people at various age levels learn in different ways and have different interests and activity preferences than people at other age levels. However, complete segmentation robs the body of the richness of intergenerational interaction. In almost every area of life, children and adults function separately and, in many cases, rightly so. But functioning separately is not enough. An important role of the pastor in ministry with children and youth, especially with today's Millennial Generation, is to ensure that programs and activities are designed to include intentional inter-generational bridge building.

One example of this type of programming is seen in the way we designed a recent stewardship program in my church. There were, of course, sermons, mailings, and witness moments from lay people. In addition, though, we did more for the children than to simply provide them with a lesson on giving and a little bank to fill in. We created a workbook to be used by parents and children together during the whole period of the stewardship emphasis. Parents and children were to work together on daily activities. The themes in the workbook corresponded to the themes developed in the worship services. The workbook had questions to be discussed, pictures to be drawn, prayers to be prayed, Bible stories to be read, and a song to be learned at home. We included a cassette tape in the packet so that the parents and children could learn the song together as they drove to soccer practice or to the store.

The children's stewardship packet provided a vehicle to facilitate the interaction between adult and child. In this interaction not only did the children learn from the adults but the adults also learned from the children. Adults were placed in a position of being the ones who had to be clear enough about their own beliefs to be able to articulate the values of stewardship to their children. The activity/reflection packet was the roux that created the context in which the adults seasoned the children and the children seasoned the adults. The intentional interaction created a richness that would have been impossible otherwise. Intentional bridge building is not in itself a program, but it is a value that needs always to be present when planning for and ordering the life of the congregation.

An Adventure Toward Hope

Ministry with the Millennial Generation is an incarnational adventure. It is not that we are called simply to use child-appropriate language and educational methods, but we must be prepared to enter incarnationally into the life of a child, youth, or young adult. But minister, teacher, parent, beware: When we enter the world of a Millennial, we enter what is for many who are older a whole new reality, a whole new world. It is a world of activity and information, a world of complexity and emotion, a world of pain and privilege, and a world of niche marketing and stimulation.

We enter the world of the Millennial Generation not only to offer them Jesus but also to learn from the Jesus in them. Whether we realize it or not, the world around us is changing dramatically and quickly. The shape of the church will also change as it interacts with this emerging world, and the Millennial Generation will play a large part in creating the emerging church. As I have come to know many of the Millennials in my congregation, I have seen in them some powerful gifts they can and will offer the church and the world. As I get to know these young ones, I see spiritual depth and a hunger to grow in relationship with God. I see a strong passion for what is right, from ecological to interpersonal issues. I see an openness to inclusiveness

Pointers for Pastors

- Learn about the toys, games, books, movies, videos, and activities of Millennials.

- Analyze your sermons: Do they include references that speak to each generation in your worshiping community?

- Attend school and community events where Millennials are present.

- Include Millennials of all ages in leadership in worship.

- Make sure church-wide events include Millennials.

- Meet with a group of Millennials at least three times a year to find out what issues they are facing. Find out what they are seeing and reading. Ask how the church can be a place where they would invite their friends.

- Be an advocate for the children, youth, and young adults in your church and community.

as a lifestyle. I see a desire to be faithful to the core of their heritage. I see a willingness to live faith beyond the walls of the church. I see a familiarity and a level of comfort with the complex technologies that seem so foreign to many in previous generations. And as I see these things, I see that they offer the church a hope-filled future.

And Now It Starts!

Craig Kennet Miller

My assignment was clear. I was to watch nine nieces and nephews along with my daughter while my wife, her sister, and her mother went shopping. With children ranging from ages three to twelve, I wondered how I would be able to take care of all of them at the same time. It was a summer vacation moment that I knew I had to prepare for. So, I went to Toys "R" Us and armed myself with two sure-fire tools, a deck of cards and the game UNO. I was positive a round of spoons and some games of UNO would eat up the time and keep the kids busy before things got out of control.

When I arrived for my assigned mission, I found out how out of touch I really am. The eleven-year-old boy had his Nintendo hooked up to his grandmother's TV, and the group was divided into teams as they competed with each other. Two other boys, ages eight and nine, were sitting on the couch with their Game Boys.

To their credit, they played one game of UNO, but that was all they could put up with. As one of my nephews explained, "This is boring."

After I explained to them that I could not get ten kids into my car to go see a movie, they were satisfied with a rented movie and a bucket of popcorn.

Another piece of information to finish out the picture might be helpful. These all-American kids were second-generation Chinese-Americans. However, when it was time to eat, Chinese food was not on the menu. Pizza, tacos, and ribs were the foods of choice.

All of this is to say that as much as we may think we know, the world of Millennials is a foreign land to most of us. The challenge for the church is to discover how to develop relationships with Millennials so that we can learn about their world and, in turn, give to them the good news of Jesus Christ.

The one theme that runs through all the articles in this book is that developing relationships with Millennials is the key. This is no secret. At each time of generational change, churches make choices about how they will interact with the newest generation. Throughout history, the Christian faith has been passed from one generation to the next through the willingness of an older generation to live their lives and express their faith in relationship with the youngest among them.

Our greatest legacy as Christians, and as individuals, will be found in our willingness to be in ministry with the Millennial Generation. The harvest is plentiful. At no time in the world's history have there been so many people under the age of fifteen. Today, thirty percent of the world's population, more than 1.8 billion, are under the age of fifteen.

As we look to the future, time is of the essence. Before I know it, my nephews and nieces and my daughter will be graduating from high school and moving on with their lives. My hope is that in their time of adolescence, they will make a connection with God that will last a lifetime.

So, where do we start? We start with prayer, a prayer that God will show us how to listen and respond to the needs of our children, youth, and young adults. We start by humbling ourselves to say that we do not have all the answers, but that we have a willingness to serve. We say to God that we are willing to do whatever it takes to make our witness so real and compelling that Jesus Christ can touch the hearts and souls of our young people, that they might know what it is to be loved by the one who was willing to give his life for them.

So, the invitation to you is this: Pray, listen, and serve in the name of the one who promises us eternal life. That is where it starts. Amen.

Study Guide

MaryJane Pierce Norton

This study guide is provided to help you better learn things you need to know about the Millennial Generation from this book. The study guide may be used with

- parent groups
- administrative groups in the church
- small groups of interested adults
- Millennials themselves, particularly older youth and young adults
- individuals interested in personal reflection.

Session Length: 60–75 minutes

Session Format: Each session will follow a common format:

- Scripture study
- an activity for moving into the material
- a summary of material for the leader's talk
- discussion questions for leading the group
- a closing time of prayer

Supplies Needed for Each Session

For each participant

- Bible
- copy of *Making God Real for a New Generation*
- pens or pencils
- plain sheets of writing paper

For the leader

- Bible
- copy of *Making God Real for a New Generation*
- newsprint and wide-tip markers
- tape or pushpins for posting written material

Session One: Who Are the Millennials?

Scripture (10 minutes)

Read aloud together Psalm 144:12-15. Allow about five minutes of silence for participants to reflect individually on what the words of the Scripture say to them about their hopes and dreams for the youth of today.

Then say: "The psalmist reminds us of the many good ways we hope our youth will grow. Our desire for any generation is that they will grow in the ways of God and successfully navigate the world. This book, *Making God Real for a New Generation,* helps us focus on what we need to know in order to better understand the unique desires and needs of the Millennial Generation."

Activity (15–20 minutes)

In order to illustrate the different generational types, use the chart on page 13. Invite participants to stand as you call out their birth years. Then ask each group to name some of the unique things they have experienced because of being born when they were born.

Have the group line up from oldest to youngest. Then invite them to pair up and tell each other one thing they hope they can pass onto other generations in their congregation.

Allow volunteers to tell what they have talked about. List these hopes and dreams on newsprint, and then post them in the room.

Summary (10–15 minutes)

Ask everyone to be seated again. Present the summary either orally, by key points written on newsprint or on an overhead projector, or by a PowerPoint presentation. Tell participants that you are summarizing the material found in "Who Are the Millennials?," Section One in the book *Making God Real for a New Generation.* Invite the participants to turn to page 11 in the book and to follow along as you speak.

Summary Notes: In Section One, "Who Are the Millennials?," readers are introduced to the concepts of generational theory and what markers we see at this time influencing the Millennial Generation (those born from 1982 to 1999). Much of what forms generational identity takes place in the youth boom of that generation. A youth boom hits when a generation is ages seven to twenty-four. For the Millennials, the youth boom will hit in the years 2006 to 2012. We are just beginning to gather data and examine this generation.

As we decipher what influences this generation of children and youth, we need to pay attention to the following seven characteristics:

- The sheer numbers of this generation can be overwhelming. It is the largest generation yet in our nation.
- The push to succeed, to excel, and to be the best is part of our culture. Keeping in mind the numbers, it will be difficult for all to succeed. And we have to ask, "Who defines success?"
- Gender issues exist. What boys do, what girls do, and how they do it becomes an issue in school, in activities, in college.
- Experience-based living is the norm. Our culture looks for, claims, and thrives on experience. Life is art.
- Our children, youth, and young adults are multiethnic. Ethnic groups are growing, but, even more so, our multiethnic populations are growing.
- Fear surrounds us. We live in a world of violence, of uncertainty, and of locked doors with no sense of security.
- Relationships are key.

Questions for Discussion (20–25 minutes)

Following the summary, invite the group to participate in a discussion time. If you have more than eight people in your group, divide the group into smaller groups of from four to six people. Introduce each question, allow for discussion, and then take comments in the larger group before moving to the next question.

1. What most excites you about this generation of children, youth, and young adults?

2. What are some of your biggest worries about this generation of children, youth, and young adults?

3. Where is your congregation doing a good job in reaching this generation of children, youth, and young adults?

4. Where does your congregation need to improve or start new efforts to reach this generation of children, youth, and young adults?

Closing Prayer (5 minutes)

Ask for a sharing of joys and concerns. Note these and ask group members to remember these prayer concerns in the time before you meet again. End by praying your own prayer or the following:

> Gracious God, we are a people in need of your guidance. We see the beauty of the world you created and are awed by its majesty. We stand with hands held out to catch the blessings you have showered into our lives, and we are thankful. We look at the precious lives of our children and youth that you have entrusted to our care, and we are both joyous and fearful. Help us honor and respect these ones who are younger than we are. Help us experience and show to others a faith that sustains, nourishes, and guides us. Help us be open to grow and change in order to continue being the vital growing body. In Christ's name we pray. Amen.

Session Two: Millennials and Their Families

Scripture (10 Minutes)

Read aloud together Ephesians 5:21–6:4. Allow about five minutes of silence for participants to reflect individually on what the words of the Scripture say to them about families.

Then say: "This passage may be familiar to you. Sometimes it is used as a tool to repress different people in the family. But the real intention here is mutual respect. At the heart of healthy relationships within the family is an atmosphere that fosters mutual respect from adult to child, from child to adult, from adult to adult, and from child to child."

Activity (15–20 minutes)

Ask each participant to draw a picture of his or her family. Do not give direction as to whether you mean people in their current household, their birth family, or church family. Simply let people select what they will draw. Allow no more than five minutes.

Invite participants to stand up, show their pictures, and talk about their families. When the group has finished, together make a list of the different kinds of families you have heard about—or know from your congregation. Include single without children, single with children, married with children, multigenerational, and so forth.

Summary (10–15 minutes)

Note that you are now moving into the summary of material for "Millennials and Their Families," Section Two in the book *Making God Real for a New Generation*. Present the summary either orally, by key points written on newsprint or on an overhead projector, or by a PowerPoint presentation. Invite the participants to turn to page 27 in the book and to follow along as you speak.

Summary Notes: One of the major influences on the growth of children and youth (and, in fact, all people) is the family. Through this section, we seek to identify the healthy ways people grow and develop, the hurts and ills that make it difficult for members of families to grow, and those things that may substitute for healthy families. The major points in this section include

- Children and youth are part of many kinds of families. The beginning point for us in working with the Millennial Generation is to pay attention to the various types of families that nurture these young people. They cannot be grouped into one family type.

- Children, youth, and young adults develop and grow with some predictability. Understanding this development is helpful in parenting and in joining in ministry with children, youth, and young adults. In this section, we see common age concerns, anticipated growth, and faith needs.

- At the heart of healthy families are healthy relationships. How we nurture relationships in families and what we do in congregations can either enhance or hinder successful living.

- Families today face many major crises. Whether it is teen pregnancy, a life-threatening illness, or violence in the home, families often have hurts and could use the help of a caring congregation.

- Just as we grow and develop as individuals, those who are parents grow through different phases of parenthood. One challenge for the church is providing appropriate parent education as it relates to the way children, teens, and young adults grow.
- When there is no healthy family, individuals seek a place of belonging, of care, and of respect outside the home. For some children, teens, and young adults, this leads to pseudo-families.
- The congregation operates as an extension of the family (as well as a body operating as the family of God). When the congregation pays attention to its role as family, it answers the needs for affirmation, community, and purpose in individuals.

Questions for Discussion (20–25 minutes)

Following the summary, invite the group to participate in a discussion time. If you have more than eight people in your group, divide the group into smaller groups of from four to six people. Introduce each question, allow for discussion, and then take comments in the larger group before moving to the next question.

1. Why, do you think, is it important to understand human growth and development?

2. What are some of the family needs you hear in your congregation?

3. How does what the church does or does not do encourage youth to stay a part of the total church family instead of drawing apart to themselves?

4. What kind of parent education and parent support would be helpful to you or to those you know in your congregation?

Closing Prayer (5 minutes)

Ask for a sharing of joys and concerns. Note these and ask group members to remember these prayer concerns in the time before you meet again. End by praying your own prayer or the following:

> Creator God, you have given us this thing called family. Sometimes this is a place of healing and support. Sometimes this is a place of hurt and violence. We know that your vision is for families to be places of mutual respect, love, and care. Help us pay attention to our families who are hurting. Help us support our families to live in healthy relationships so that all may grow in wisdom and stature and in harmony with your plans. In Christ's name we pray. Amen.

Session Three: Millennials and Their World

Scripture (10 minutes)

Read aloud together Zechariah 8:1-8. Allow about five minutes of silence for participants to reflect individually on what they hear in the Scripture about a world where children are safe.

Then say: "You may never have read these words in Zechariah. This is not a book of the Bible to which we readily turn. But this is a beautiful image of God caring for people. We have the old who sit in the streets and the young who play in the streets. When people can do that, the world is a safe place. Everyone wants a safe world for their children and youth. Everyone wants a place where children and youth can grow successfully and well. Zechariah reminds us that God is our hope for such a world."

Activity (15–20 minutes)

Give each participant a blank sheet of paper. Ask the group to number from one to ten. Say: "This is a word association game. I will read a word or phrase to you. Write down the first word or phrase that comes to your mind. Ready? Start writing."
- Divorce
- Drugs
- Religion
- Culture
- Stereotypes
- Media
- Sexuality
- Violence
- Diversity
- Plugged-in

Ask for a volunteer to be the recorder. Instruct the volunteer to write on newsprint the words from the original list and then to write the words the group members thought when they heard the words. After the group lists the words, take a few minutes to study the list the group has created.

Summary (10–15 minutes)

Move into the summary. Present the summary either orally, by key points written on newsprint or on an overhead projector, or by a PowerPoint presentation. Direct the participants to the material found in "Millennials and Their World," Section Three in the book *Making God Real for a New Generation.* Invite the participants to turn to page 69 in the book and to follow along as you speak.

Summary Notes: This may be the most difficult section in the book to understand. While we might like to separate our children and youth from the world, they live in this world and are influenced by what goes on in it. Some of the issues facing children, youth, and young adults in the culture are included here. Others are woven into the sections on family, on spirituality, and on models of ministry. Those included in this section are illustrative of the strains and dangers of the culture in which we live today.

- Kelly's diary provides an intimate view into the world of a Millennial. The issues Kelly writes about in her diary are not unique to her. We hear of drug abuse and alcohol use. We read of divorce. We see some of the uncertainties of dealing with a family. We hear about school, cliques, and talk that goes on from teen to teen.

- "The 411 on My Generation" gives an intimate view of the world through the eyes of a middle-school girl. We see how happenings in her world influence her actions, thoughts, and feelings about family, friends, and the world way beyond the occurrence of a single event.

- Children, youth, and young adults who are bridging from one culture to another face some unique concerns. We have many in this situation from a variety of backgrounds. In each, the division from the older generation by language, custom, and practice creates family strains, congregational stress, and feelings on the part of the young people of never fitting in entirely in either world.

- When people think of their youthful years, they often define that time by the music they sang, danced to, and played. Music is a defining part of the Millennials' world. Listening to the music of youth gives us a window into their needs and concerns. It might not always be the music we would wish to hear, but it does provide key information for who youth are and what they hope to be.

- We are created wonderfully and beautifully by God. A healthy approach to sexuality is a great gift to our young people. This means recognizing the images of sexuality fostered in our culture and offering a counter-culture approach.

- Our culture today seeks to own young people in many ways. Key is the focus on advertising and enticement for young people to spend money. While the world becomes more and more sophisticated and glitzy, the church could fall into the trap of competing at that level for the attention of children, youth, and young adults. We cannot compete. But we can offer meaningful relationships, with God and with others.

Questions for Discussion (20–25 minutes)

Following the summary, invite the group to participate in a discussion time. If you have more than eight people in your group, divide the group into smaller groups of from four to six people. Introduce each question, allow for discussion, and then take comments in the larger group before moving to the next question.

1. What are the issues you hear from children and youth concerning sexuality?

2. How, do you think, are children and youth today influenced by such things as movies, computers, electronic games, and print advertisements?

3. What evidences of multiculturalism do you see in your community and in your congregation?

4. What are some ways you would name for allowing times of listening to the concerns of children, youth, and young adults?

Closing Prayer (5 minutes)

Ask for a sharing of joys and concerns. Note these and ask group members to remember these prayer concerns in the time before you meet again. End by praying your own prayer or the following:

O God, who loves us all, help us listen to our children and youth. We know there are hard issues in their world. They are tempted to early experimentation with sex, to try drugs and alcohol, to seek the approval of peers or adults who may not echo the values we feel. We place in your hands our children and youth. But we also seek your guidance so that we can be available to them as parents and teachers and friends. Open our hearts and minds so that we may ask for help when we need it, provide a listening ear when called to do so, and offer guidance for healthy living. In Christ's name we pray. Amen."

Session Four: The Spirituality of Millennials

Scripture (10 minutes)

Read aloud together Deuteronomy 6:1-9. Allow about five minutes of silence for participants to reflect individually on the words of the Scripture and what this says about our responsibility for passing on the faith to our children, youth, and young adults.

Then say: "All through the Book of Deuteronomy there are admonitions to tell the children about the faith. For the Hebrew people, it was important to put into place a plan for passing on the stories of the faith from one generation to the next. Such a plan is equally important today. If we think our faith is important—that it gives direction and meaning to our lives—then we are called upon to provide ways for our young people to experience that faith."

Activity (15–20 minutes)

Depending on the size of your group, subdivide them into pairs or trios so that you can cover these four topics:
- Scripture
- Prayer
- Rituals and Traditions
- Service

Assign one topic to each group. Hand each group a marker and a sheet of newsprint. Give each group the following instruction: "On the newsprint provided, list five ways we teach or nurture this item in the home and five ways we teach or nurture this item in the congregation. Put a star by the ones you think we do the best."

When all groups are finished, ask one person from each group to post their newsprint. Invite the larger group to add to the lists that were started.

Summary (10–15 minutes)

Now move into the summary of "The Spirituality of Millennials," Section Four in the book *Making God Real for a New Generation.* Present the summary either orally, by key points written on newsprint or on an overhead projector, or by a PowerPoint presentation. Invite the participants to turn to page 97 in the book and to follow along as you speak.

Summary Notes: In some ways, this section of the book is at the heart of the questions we may have regarding ministry with the Millennial Generation. Some of the articles point to differences of this generation; others echo age-old concerns and strategies. As you listen, think about yourself when you were a child or youth. What of the following would have been true for your generation? What of the following would not have been true for your generation?

- In leading children and youth to God, we always begin with family. The faith of the hearth has the most influence on children and youth. We focus on prayer, storytelling, rituals and traditions, and service to others as paths that help children, youth, and young adults find God.

- Young people wonder about how they will know when they are responding to God's will. "Discerning God's

Will" (pages 103–6) is one young person's reflection on the process that included exploring a topic, gathering information, praying, journaling, and relying on friends to give guidance to her decision.

- The opportunity for many young people to begin reflecting on the place of God in their own lives comes through life experiences. These might sometimes be classified as crises (such as the death of a peer). At other times, the experience might simply be a point of maturity (taking part in a youth retreat). Astute leaders will be aware of these life events and help young people reflect on God at these turning points in their lives.

- Out of recent times of crisis, youth are looking for a sense of salvation, a sense of the meaning of life. For youth, salvation always comes in relationships.

- Of particular note for the Millennial Generation is service to others. A unique characteristic of this generation is the banding together for common solutions to make a difference.

- "What Is Success?" may seem like a strange article to have in the spirituality section, but ways we view success do influence both the value we place on spirituality and the time we allow for spirituality. Bombarded by many images of success, young people may be confused about what will create a successful life. The church seeks to redefine success so that young people see these components of successful lives: strong families, healthy relationships, security, discernment tools and skills, coping skills, exposure to different cultures, asset development, leader development, access to technology, advocacy, and spirituality.

Questions for Discussion (20–25 minutes)

Following the summary, invite the group to participate in a discussion time. If you have more than eight people in your group, divide the group into smaller groups of from four to six people. Introduce each question, allow time for discussion, and then take comments in the larger group before moving to the next question.

1. What spiritual disciplines and habits do you think your children and youth are being taught at home and/or at church?

2. Where are there opportunities for children, youth, and young adults to live out their faith in service in the congregation and in the community?

3. Think of your congregation. Who would you list as disciples who help others follow Jesus by the way they live their lives and reflect their faith?

4. What are the rituals and traditions that you provide in your homes and congregations to help pass on the faith?

Closing Prayer (5 minutes)

Ask for a sharing of joys and concerns. Note these and ask group members to remember these prayer concerns in the time before you meet again. End by praying your own prayer or the following:

> Gracious God, we so want a vibrant faith for ourselves and for our children, youth, and young adults. Sometimes we see that faith as a wonderful vaccination against the evils they may confront. At other times, we see it is a safe place in the midst of violence and fear. And we also know that our faith is one that will confront us and push us to seek your will. It would be so nice if we could gift wrap our faith and hand it to the next generation. But we know that is not the way faith works. Help us seize the opportunities given to us for witnessing to our faith, for providing experiences and places for our young people to question, experience, and practice faith. Amen.

Session Five: Models for Ministry With Millennials

Scripture (10 minutes)
Read aloud together John 6:1-14. Allow about five minutes of silence for participants to reflect individually on what the Scripture says to them about the ministry of the child.

Then say: "This is one of the few examples in Scripture where a child is involved directly in ministry. The child had the food. The child gave the food to Jesus. Because of the child's gift, all were fed. Often, we think about the ways we can minister *to* children and youth. This Scripture gives us an example of ministry *with* children and youth."

Activity (15–20 minutes)
Distribute to all group members a blank sheet of paper. Post the following questions:

- What is your favorite hymn or church song?
- What is your most memorable worship service?
- What Sunday school or small-group study has had the most influence on you?
- What rites of passage or church rituals do you remember from your childhood and teen years?

Call out each question, and ask the participants to write down their answer. Then ask the group, "Were there any surprises to you in what you remembered? What made a hymn, worship service, ritual, or study memorable for you? What does that say to you about what our children, youth, and young adults might need from the church?"

Summary (10–15 minutes)
Move into the summary of material "Models for Ministry With Millennials," Section Five in *Making God Real for a New Generation*. Present the summary either orally, by key points written on newsprint or on an overhead projector, or by a PowerPoint presentation. Invite the participants to turn to page 125 in the book and to follow along as you speak.

Summary Notes: There is no one recipe for ministry with Millennials. Presented in this section are some models that take into consideration their needs and desires.

- Building a discipleship system sets forth a plan for the congregation. It asks us to consider how we introduce the faith, teach the faith, help people claim the faith, and aid people in acting out of faith.

- One of the key places for involvement in the congregation is corporate worship. Of course, we are not seeking a one-generation worship service but are looking at the ways we weave together traditions to involve everyone.

- Another key place for involvement in the congregation is small groups. Children are most likely to be part of small groups through the Sunday school. Youth and young adults are moving to other types of small groups. In all of these places, the central question is, How do these groups nurture individuals for study, prayer, story, and ministry to others?

- Recognizing the importance of rites of passage and establishing these markers of growth and responsibility in church life may be a challenge for congregations. With a rite of passage, there are three steps: separation of who/what a person has been, initiation into who the person is becoming, and reincorporation into the community. Young people like and need rites of passage to recognize growth and to receive added responsibility.

- Another model of ministry looks at ways congregations can become multiethnic. Remember, this is one of the markers of the Millennial Generation. But it takes hard work to reach out to those who are different. Becoming multiethnic means giving up some of who we are as well as adding and growing in new ways. Sometimes this means going outside the walls of the church.

- The pastor is an important part of helping Millennials feel accepted and wanted in the church. In the article "The Pastor's Role With Millennials," the author uses the image of pitching a tent in the world to remind us that we have to listen to, be with, and stand by Millennials. In addition, this points us to the importance, even as we learn about one generation, to be multigenerational in our approach to ministry.

Questions for Discussion (20–25 minutes)
Following the summary, invite the group to participate in a discussion time. If you have more than eight people in your group, divide the group into smaller groups of from four to six people. Introduce each question, allow for discussion, and then take comments in the larger group before moving to the next question.

1. What about your worship service invites the involvement of young people?

2. What about your worship service excludes young people?

3. Reflect on the four steps in discipleship:

   a. Introducing people to faith

   b. Learning about faith traditions

   c. Claiming the faith

   d. Acting out of faith

4. Reflect on the different parts of ministry with young people in your congregation. What enables each of these to happen?

5. How would groups of young people or people in your community who are different from you (economically, culturally, racially) feel included in your congregation?

Closing Prayer (5 minutes)

Ask for a sharing of joys and concerns. Note these and ask group members to remember these prayer concerns. End by praying your own prayer or the following:

God of us all, we thank you for the opportunity to engage in study together. We thank you for the ways we have learned from one another in this time of study. Help us be open to the ways we can minister to and with our young people. Help us listen clearly and plan wisely. Remind us constantly that the relationships we form and nurture with our young people are key to their understandings of themselves, of others, and of you. In the name of Jesus Christ, our Lord and Savior. Amen.

00000—1982/1999—00000

Millennial Generation Survey, 2002

The General Board of Discipleship

00000—1982/1999—0

Millennial Generation Survey, 2002

The General Board of Discipleship

This survey was conducted by the Center for Evangelism Through New Congregational Development at the General Board of Discipleship of The United Methodist Church in February 2002. The participants included 500 high school students in public high schools in California, Florida, Alabama, Louisiana, Illinois, Maryland, Mississippi, Ohio, Pennsylvania, New Jersey, South Carolina, Texas, and Wisconsin.

Survey questions are based on youth surveys of 1993 and 1995. The results of those previous surveys are documented in the book *Postmoderns: The Beliefs, Hopes, and Fears of Young Americans,* by Craig Kennet Miller (Discipleship Resources, 1997).

For comprehensive results that break down the survey information by age, gender, and ethnicity, contact Craig Kennet Miller at cmiller@gbod.org.

Participants = 500

Gender   54% Female   46% Male

Grade   24% 9th   23% 10th   32% 11th   21% 12th

Grade Point   2% 2.0   9% 2.5   24% 3.0   39% 3.5   26% 4.0

Racial-Ethnic Group

62%	Euro-American	6%	Asian American/Pacific Islander/Native Hawaiian
15%	African American	4%	Multiethnic
12%	Hispanic/Latino American	1%	Native American

If multiethnic, check boxes that apply:

53%	Euro-American	32%	Asian American
47%	African American	32%	Native American
37%	Hispanic/Latino American	11%	Pacific Islander/Native Hawaiian

English is your: 87% Native language   13% Second language

Family income: 9% Lower income   77% Middle income   14% Upper income

Parents' birth: 80% In U.S.A.   14% Outside U.S.A.   6% One born outside U.S.A.

Your birth: 91% In U.S.A.   9% Outside U.S.A.

What is your current family situation?

- 63% Live with both biological parents
- 16% Blended family
- 13% Single-parent mom
- 2% Joint Custody
- 2% Single-parent dad
- 4% Other

Which political party do you most identify with?

- 44% Democrat
- 37% Republican
- 17% Independent
- 1% Undecided
- 1% Other

1. Which of the following have you experienced?

78%   Having a great coach or teacher
71%   Being on a winning team
61%   Baptism/Confirmation
55%   Having a close friend of another race
55%   Death of a grandparent
50%   A religious experience
30%   Losing your virginity
29%   Death of a close friend
24%   Your parents' divorce
21%   Counseling or therapy
20%   Parent losing a job
19%   A parent's wedding
15%   A parent's serious illness
10%   Addiction to drugs or alcohol
10%   Your own suicide attempt
7%   Physical or sexual abuse
5%   Death of a parent or a brother/sister
5%   Victim of a violent crime
3%   Having a baby

2. Which had the most impact?

15%   A religious experience
13%   Having a great coach or teacher
12%   Your parents' divorce
12%   Death of a grandparent
8%   Baptism/Confirmation
8%   Death of a close friend
7%   Being on a winning team
4%   Death of a parent or a brother/sister
3%   A parent's serious illness
3%   Losing your virginity
3%   Having a close friend of another race
3%   Your own suicide attempt
3%   Parent losing a job
2%   A parent's wedding
2%   Addiction to drugs or alcohol
2%   Physical or sexual abuse
1%   Counseling or therapy
0%   Victim of a violent crime
0%   Having a baby

3. Are you involved in one or more of the following activities?

57%   The arts
53%   Organized sports
49%   Religious youth group (church, synagogue, temple, and so forth)
43%   Work part-time
40%   Service organization or club at school
24%   Youth organizations

4. Have you ever?

- 77% Cheated on a test
- 65% Flown in a plane
- 36% Drank to get drunk
- 30% Viewed porn on the Net
- 29% Gambled
- 27% Lived in a different state
- 24% Traveled overseas
- 19% Smoked pot
- 14% Tried illegal drugs
- 14% Regularly smoked cigarettes

5. Which of the following do you have in your home?

- 91% Computer
- 87% Cable TV
- 85% Internet access

6. Which of the following do you have in your bedroom?

- 85% Television
- 55% Cable or satellite TV
- 40% Computer
- 29% Internet access

7. Which of the following do you carry with you?

- 70% Cell phone
- 47% CD player
- 10% Pager
- 8% Palm Pilot or similar device
- 6% Game Boy or similar device
- 3% Personal alarm

8. Which do you most often do when you have free time? (pick three)

- 49% Connect with friends
- 46% Watch TV
- 46% Listen to music
- 28% Play sports
- 28% Play a video/computer game
- 24% Surf the Net
- 23% Watch a video or DVD
- 20% Listen to the radio
- 19% Play music
- 17% Read a book
- 13% Pray
- 11% Connect with family

9. How often do you go to religious services?

- 56% Weekly
- 14% Yearly
- 13% Never
- 9% Twice a month
- 8% Monthly

10. Where do you plan to go after high school?

- 91% College
- 4% Military
- 3% Full-time work
- 2% Trade school

11. What do you expect to achieve by the time you are thirty?

- 73% All of the following
- 19% To have a secure job
- 14% To own my own home
- 11% To be married
- 3% To have a child
- 1% None of the above

12. Other than your family or friends, which most influences the choices you make?

- 41% Church/Temple/Mosque
- 37% School
- 19% Media (TV, radio, and so forth)
- 3% Government

13. How often do you eat dinner with your parents?

- 37% 5 to 7 times a week
- 28% 3 to 4 times a week
- 24% 1 to 2 times a week
- 11% Never

14. What are your favorite kinds of music? (pick two)

- 58% Pop/Rock
- 53% Rap/Hip-Hop
- 21% Alternative
- 18% Soul/Rhythm & Blues
- 17% Country
- 11% Contemporary Inspirational/Christian/Contemporary Christian/Gospel
- 10% Classical
- 5% Latin
- 3% Metal/Classic Rock/Heavy Metal/Punk/Techno
- 4% Other

15. Which two are the greatest issues facing your generation?

- 41% Stopping drug and alcohol abuse
- 39% Stopping violence in schools and local communities
- 33% Fighting terrorism
- 28% Stopping racism and sexism
- 22% Taking care of the environment
- 20% Stopping the breakdown of the family
- 19% Fixing the education system
- 13% Fixing the economy

16. How did the events of September 11, 2001 affect you personally? (pick two)

- 44% I have more respect for the military, firefighters, and police
- 26% I am more aware of the future
- 26% I am more patriotic
- 22% I have a better appreciation of my family
- 14% I am more religious
- 14% I am afraid to fly on airplanes
- 13% It has made no difference in my life
- 11% I am more tolerant of people who are different than me
- 7% I have more trust in our government
- 6% I am more likely to vote in the future
- 5% I am more likely to choose a career that helps other people
- 4% I am less likely to live far away from home
- 3% I am less tolerant of people who are different than me

For Further Reading

Resources published by Discipleship Resources may be ordered online at www.discipleshipresources.org; by phone at 800-685-4370; by fax at 770-442-9742; or by mail from Discipleship Resources Distribution Center, PO Box 1616, Alpharetta, GA 30009-1616.

Books

Baby Boomer Spirituality: Ten Essential Values of a Generation, by Craig Kennet Miller (Nashville: Discipleship Resources, 1992). Of interest to parents and adults who work with the Millennial Generation; points out facts about the generation we call Baby Boomers.

Before They Ask: Talking With Your Child About Sex From a Christian Perspective (Revised Edition), edited by Vince Isner (Nashville: Abingdon Press, 1999). A guide for parents on children's sexual development from birth through age twelve; includes commonly asked questions and material for parents to use in answering questions.

Boys and Girls Learn Differently!: A Guide for Teachers and Parents, by Michael Gurian (San Francisco: Jossey-Bass, 2001). Includes information about how boys and girls develop, how their brains develop, and social and educational activities for boys and girls.

Building Assets in Congregations: A Practical Guide for Helping Youth Grow Up Healthy, by Eugene Roehlkepartain (Minneapolis: Search Institute, 1998). Congregational leaders can do a self-assessment and select ways to ensure the building of assets for youth.

Capture the Moment: Building Faith Traditions for Families, by Rick and Sue Isbell (Nashville: Discipleship Resources, 1998). Includes a listing of experiences in the family, with devotional suggestions and topics of discussion for use in the home.

Children Worship! by MaryJane Pierce Norton (Nashville: Discipleship Resources, 1997). Educating our children for worship is the focus of this book. Includes lesson plans, bulletin inserts, parents' letters, reproducible activity sheets, and suggestions for using the study intergenerationally as well as with children ages five through eight.

Created by God: About Human Sexuality for Older Girls and Boys (Revised Edition), by James H. Ritchie (Nashville: Abingdon Press, 1999). This is a course on human sexuality that is written for fifth and sixth graders. It includes a leader's guide with lesson plans, a CD with songs for class use and computer graphics for overheads, and a student guide that is a reading book on sexuality.

Deepening Youth Spirituality: The Youth Worker's Guide, by Walt Marcum (Nashville: Abingdon Press, 2001). Provides plans for leading youth to God through Bible study, prayer, worship, retreats, journaling.

FaithHome (Leader's Guide, Parent's Study Guide, Pastor's Guide, Video) (Nashville: Abingdon Press). Emphasizes home-based faith formation, supported by weekly church sessions over a nine-week period.

FaithHome for Parents (Nashville: Abingdon Press). Twenty-two quick-reading booklets addressed to parents. Topics include prayer, communication, discipline, anger, substance abuse, divorce, grief, time management.

FaithHome for Parents Group Study Guide, by Lynn Hutton (Nashville: Abingdon Press, 2001). Information for leaders of parent groups using twelve of the *FaithHome for Parents* booklets.

Family, the Forming Center: A Vision of the Role of Family in Spiritual Formation (Revised Edition), by Marjorie J. Thompson (Nashville: Upper Room, 1997). Provides a solid grounding for the importance of the family in forming faith.

The First Three Years: A Guide for Ministry With Infants, Toddlers, and Two-Year-Olds, edited by Mary Alice Gran (Nashville, Discipleship Resources, 2001). Includes information about childcare, recruiting and training workers, parent education, proper hiring practices, child development, and more.

The Five Love Languages: How to Express Heartfelt Commitment to Your Mate, by Gary Chapman (Chicago: Northfield Publishing, 1992). Helpful in learning to understand the significant people in a person's life, as well as learning to speak their language so that they feel loved.

The Godbearing Life: The Art of Soul-Tending for Youth Ministry, by Kenda Creasy Dean and Ron Foster (Nashville: Upper Room, 1998). A spiritual primer and practical guide for those who pastor young people.

Hand in Hand: Growing Spiritually With Our Children, by Sue Downing (Nashville: Discipleship Resources, 1998). Serves well as a gift book to new parents, with information on prayer, reading the Bible, participating in worship, establishing faith traditions, and dealing with crises with children.

Helping Children Cope With Divorce, by Jenni Douglas Duncan (Nashville; Discipleship Resources, 1999). A guide for congregations; contains sessions for children whose parents have divorced.

The Hero's Journey: Joseph Campbell on His Life and Work, by Joseph Campbell, edited by Phil Cousineau (New York: Harper-Collins-UK, 1999). Joseph Campbell has helped generations of leaders reflect on the importance of story, of ritual, and of passages in finding meaning in life.

Integrating Service Learning and Multicultural Education in Colleges and Universities, edited by Carolyn R. O'Grady (Mahwah, NJ: Lawrence Erlbaum Associates, 2000). Resource and guide for service-learning practitioners committed to contributing substantively to community-defined needs.

Keeping in Touch: Christian Formation and Teaching, by Carol F. Krau (Nashville: Discipleship Resources, 1999). Guides teachers and leaders through keeping in touch with God, with God's people, with their own experience, with the world, and with teaching.

Let's Be Real: Honest Discussions About Faith and Sexuality (Abingdon Press, 1998). This resource addresses issues concerning youth sexuality and gives several models for learning experiences with youth in grades six through twelve.

Managing Generation X: How to Bring Out the Best in Young Talent (Revised and Updated), by Bruce Tulgan (New York: W.W. Norton & Company, 2000). Points to aspects of work ethic differences from one generation to another.

Millennials Rising: The Next Great Generation, by Neil Howe and William Strauss (New York: Vintage Books, 2000). A demographic look at the Millennial Generation.

The Multigenerational Congregation: Meeting the Leadership Challenge, by Gil Rendle (Bethesda, MD: The Alban Institute, 2002). Pays attention to generational needs and helps leaders in creating congregations where multiple generations feel included, wanted, and involved.

NextChurch.Now: Creating New Faith Communities, by Craig Kennet Miller (Nashville: Discipleship Resources, 2000). Includes generational information and an examination of components of worship and congregational life, with the purpose of aiding congregations to reach out to those in their communities seeking God.

Now Is the Time!: Ministry With the Millennial Generation Born From 1982 to 1999, by Craig Kennet Miller (Nashville: Discipleship Resources, 1999). This video and 16-page leader's guide introduces the Millennial Generation (video: 7 minutes, 42 seconds).

Out of the Basement: A Holistic Approach to Children's Ministry, by Diane C. Olson (Nashville: Discipleship Resources, 2001). Diane Olson guides children's ministry planners and leaders through building a congregational system for supporting children as they grow as disciples.

Parents and Grandparents as Spiritual Guides: Nurturing Children of the Promise, by Betty Shannon Cloyd (Nashville: Upper Room, 2000). Explores the simple ways parents and grandparents can introduce children to the presence of God and nurture them spiritually.

Postmoderns: The Beliefs, Hopes, and Fears of Young Americans (1965-1981), by Craig Kennet Miller (Nashville: Discipleship Resources, 1997). For those seeking more information on the Postmodern Generation (those born from 1965 to 1981); provides information on nine culture shifts that shaped the generation.

PowerXPress (Nashville: Abingdon Press). Children's curriculum that provides all that is needed to set up the learning stations.

Real Teens: A Contemporary Snapshot of Youth Culture, by George Barna (Ventura, CA: Regal Books, 2001). Based on survey information, gives information on lifestyles, what teens are thinking and feeling, faith and spirituality, racial and ethnic perspectives.

Safe Sanctuaries: Reducing the Risk of Child Abuse in the Church, by Joy Thornburg Melton (Nashville: Discipleship Resources, 1998). Helps congregations create places of safety for children and youth; contains helpful forms, policies, and procedures.

The Secret Life of the Brain, by Richard Restak, M.D. (Washington, D.C.: Joseph Henry Press and The Dana Press, 2001). Along with the PBS video series, *The Secret Life of the Brain* provides guidance to the most recent findings in brain development.

Side by Side: Families Learning and Living the Faith Together, by Delia Halverson (Nashville: Abingdon Press, 2002). Sunday school lessons designed for intergenerational use; children and parents can learn together.

Soul Tending: Life-Forming Practices for Older Youth and Young Adults (Nashville: Abingdon Press, 2002). Guides youth, young adults, and adults through spiritual formation experiences.

The Spectacle of Worship in a Wired World: Electronic Culture and the Gathered People of God, by Tex Sample (Nashville: Abingdon Press, 1998). Examines three elements of electronic culture (images, sound as beat, and visualization) and looks at ways these are already in worship and at ways they might be incorporated into worship in order to reach those born since 1945.

Spirit of the Child, by David Hay with Rebecca Nye (Grand Rapids: Zondervan Publishing House, 1998). Written out of interviews with British children, explores the natural spirituality of children.

Talking With Your Child: Conversations for Life, edited by Rebecca Laird (Nashville: Abingdon Press, 1999) and *Talking With Your Teen: Conversations for Life,* edited by Lynn Hutton (Nashville: Abingdon Press, 1999). Parenting education curriculum that includes a leader's guide and a parent book. Topics include communication, respect, feelings, success and failure, grief, sexuality.

Twists of Faith: Ministry With Youth at the Turning Points of Their Lives, by Marcey Balcomb and Kevin Witt (Nashville: Discipleship Resources, 1999). Examines what happens to youth when events and circumstances create turning points in their lives; includes devotional material and strategies for connecting turning points with faith experiences.

United Methodist Youth Handbook, by Micheal Selleck (Nashville: Discipleship Resources, 1999). Provides information for beginning and maintaining a congregational youth ministry that helps youth grow as disciples.

The Way We Never Were: American Families and the Nostalgia Trap (Reprint Edition), by Stephanie Coontz (New York: Basic Books, 2000). An examination of the myths about family in our culture. At times caustic, the book does help give a long-term perspective on some of the ills of families.

The Way We Really Are: Coming to Terms With America's Changing Families, by Stephanie Coontz (New York: Basic Books, 1998). Places into perspective families in the United States today, including family types, specific needs, and strengths.

What Every Teacher Needs to Know About... (Nashville: Discipleship Resources, 2002). Series of ten booklets that provides Sunday school teachers and small-group leaders with basic information on such things as faith language, people, curriculum, theology, the Bible, and The United Methodist Church.

What Kids Need to Succeed: Proven, Practical Ways to Raise Good Kids (Revised and Updated Edition), by Peter L. Benson, Judy Galbraith, and Pamela Espeland (Minneapolis: Free Spirit Publishing, 1998). Identifies developmental assets kids need to lead healthy lives; for parents, teachers, youth leaders, and teens.

Why God Won't Go Away: Brain Science and the Biology of Belief, by Andrew Newberg, Eugene D'Aquili, and Vince Rause (New York: Ballantine Books, 2001). Fairly technical weaving of neurological information that attempts to understand the complex relationship between spirituality and the brain.

Workshop Rotation: A New Model for Sunday School, by Melissa Armstrong-Hansche and Neil MacQueen (Louisville: Westminster John Knox Press, 2000). A step-by-step guide for setting up and conducting the workshop rotation model.

Young Lions: Christian Rites of Passage for African American Young Men, by Chris McNair (Nashville: Abingdon Press, 2001). Offers a model for providing young men a faith passage from adolescence to adulthood.

Staff of the General Board of Discipleship and the United Methodist Youth Organization

- Terry Carty, Director, Center for Ministries With Young People
- Bill Crenshaw, Director, Ministries With Young Adults
- Drew Dyson, Executive Director, Shared Mission Focus on Young People
- Mary Alice Gran, Director, Ministries With Children
- Susan Hay, Director, Ministries With Youth
- Jan Knight, Editor, *Pockets,* The Upper Room
- Craig Kennet Miller, Director, Center of Evangelism Through New Congregational Development
- MaryJane Pierce Norton, Team Leader, Family and Life Span Ministries
- Robin Pippin, Editor, *Devo'Zine,* The Upper Room
- Soozung Sa, Director, Ministries With Singles and Families
- Ronna Seibert, Executive Director, United Methodist Youth Organization
- Kevin Witt, Director, Camping and Retreat Ministries

Helpful Websites

- The General Board of Discipleship: www.gbod.org
- Discipleship Resources: www.discipleshipresources.org
- The Upper Room: www.upperroom.org
- Cokesbury: www.cokesbury.com
  www.ileadyouth.com
  www.ilearntoteach.com
- Shared Mission Focus on Young People: www.idreamachurch.com
- Augsburg Youth and Family Institute: www.youthfamilyinstitute.com
- Barna Research Group: www.barna.org
- Children's Defense Fund: www.childrensdefense.org
- Interlinc Online (online music): www.Interlinc-online.com
- Search Institute: www.search-institute.org
- People's Cyber Nation: www.cyber-nation.com